FORMULA ONE RACE CIRCUITS

FORMULA ONE RACE CIRCUITS

EXPLORE THE WORLD'S GREATEST RACE TRACKS, INCLUDING SINGAPORE AND VALENCIA STREET CIRCUITS **MIRCO DE CET**

LORENZ BOOKS

CONTENTS

This edition is published by Lorenz Books
an imprint of Anness Publishing Ltd
Blaby Road, Wigston, Leicestershire LE18 4SE
info@anness.com

www.lorenzbooks.com; www.annesspublishing.com

Anness Publishing has a new picture agency
outlet for images for publishing, promotions
or advertising. Please visit our website
www.practicalpictures.com for more information.

© Anness Publishing Ltd 2013

A CIP catalogue record for this book
is available from the British Library.

Publisher: Joanna Lorenz
Senior Editor: Felicity Forster
Production Manager: Steve Lang

Produced for Anness Publishing Limited
   by Editorial Developments,
   Edgmond, Shropshire, England
Designer: Chensie Chen
General Editor: Quentin Daniel
Index: Marie Lorimer

PUBLISHER'S NOTE
Although the advice and information
in this book are believed to be
accurate and true at the time of
going to press, neither the authors
nor the publisher can accept
any legal responsibility or liability
for any errors or omissions that may
have been made nor for any inaccuracies
nor for any loss, harm or injury that
comes about from following instructions
or advice in this book.

INTRODUCTION

Imagine having to make yourself comfortable in a machine that can exceed 300 kph (187.5 mph). You switch on the engine and hear its earth-shattering roar – then prepare yourself to tame the blacktop ahead. You have to learn all the twists and turns that will come and go in the blink of an eye. You have to know exactly where to be when you enter the corners and judge the best position to exit. You have to drive both fast and smooth, and when you've finally mastered the circuit and all it throws at you, you have to do it again, this time for the duration of a whole race, which can be over seventy laps. You can't afford to lose concentration for a split second, otherwise the gravel trap will simply eat you up!

These are some of the challenges a race circuit poses the Formula One driver. Every circuit has its own particular character and makes its own special demands. But over the past ten years these tracks have themselves undergone huge changes. Today they almost resemble highly sophisticated theme parks. The actual motor racing is still the major event, but it's now complemented by a number of alternative sideshows and attractions. The venues too have changed dramatically, with circuits being constructed in Malaysia, Bahrain and even China. Countries that were once bemused by the sight of cars racing round a track now see it as a welcome money-spinner and a major tourist attraction. The world has shrunk; air travel has become relatively cheap and easy, and these days it's not just the rich who are happy to go halfway round the world to attend a Formula One Grand Prix.

These new complexes, many of which were designed and built by Hermann Tilke and his German group of companies, are modern, clean and replete with all kinds of facilities. They've come a very long way from the rather rough-and-ready airfield

circuits that were common just after the Second World War. Design features have been given considerable thought and close attention paid to the 'look' that would best characterize the country where each huge arena is sited. Above all, they've been designed with safety in mind – though some would say that has taken some of the thrill out of the sport. Long gone are straw bales for crash barriers – today's Formula One cars would simply fly straight through them! Run-off areas and gravel traps are well positioned and abundant, giving the cars time to slow from their exceptionally high speeds before they impact into soft barriers such as tyre walls. Overtaking is also a problem that has to be solved at many circuits, not just because of track layout but also because of the width of modern cars, their aerodynamic effect and their speed.

This book presents a colourful survey of the world's top race circuits. It shows the full extent of the changes made to the sport in recent times, and how these have affected racing in general. But while change may sometimes be controversial, and the loss of the old circuits may be sad, progress dictates that modernization and radical new design ideas must take their place in the effort to make Formula One fit for purpose in the 21st century.

BAHRAIN GRAND PRIX

Venue: Bahrain International Circuit, Manama, Kingdom of Bahrain

The Crown Prince, Shaikh Salman bin Hamad Al Khalifa, Honorary President of the Bahrain Motor Federation, instigated the building of the Bahrain Circuit as a national objective. The circuit was designed by the German architect Hermann Tilke, who has recently been involved with several other circuit designs and renovations. The place where the circuit was to be built threw up its own particular problems. Although the area is bathed in beautiful sunshine, the desert is not the ideal place to build anything! But this project, like many others carried out in this part of the world, was done with

Bahrain International Circuit

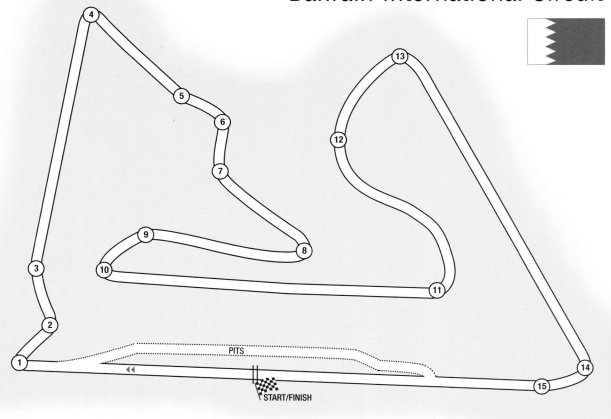

great care and attention and with the use of the latest technology and resources. One of the main concerns was that sand would be a major hazard, not only to spectators but more importantly to the drivers during the races. A solution was found, though: the sandy area around the circuit was sprayed with a special adhesive.

At one point during construction it was seriously thought that the circuit would not be finished for the scheduled race in 2004, but F1 supremo Bernie Ecclestone insisted that it would, and finished it was – well enough to stage a race anyway.

The Kingdom of Bahrain is an island group located off the central southern shores of the Arabian

The striking Sakhir Tower, now an iconic landmark, encompasses some of the most beautiful lounges and most amazing views in the Kingdom. Here Michael Schumacher leads the pack round turn 1, at the start of the 2006 race.

Gulf, between Saudi Arabia's east coast and the Qatar peninsula. There are some thirty-six islands, with a total land area of about 706 square km. Bahrain Island is the largest and its capital city is Manama. The Grand Prix circuit is located at Sakhir, some 30 km south-west of Manama, and is very accessible to both the city centre and the airport, being about a thirty minute drive from both.

The circuit incorporates six different layouts: the 5.411 km Grand Prix track as depicted on our map; the 2.55 km Inner track, situated in the middle section of the circuit, with eight turns; the 3.664 km Outer track, which joins turns four and thirteen, and has ten turns; the 3.7 km Paddock Circuit, where turns three to nine are removed; a drag strip which runs from the tower for 1,200 metres and then has a shut-down area; and finally a 2 km oval test track.

These six different layouts give a good choice when it comes to the type of racing that can be held here. Drag racing, Formula One, Formula Three, GP2 series, the Bahrain GT Festival and the V8 festival are regulars already.

The Crown Prince spearheaded a major national initiative to bring Formula One racing to Bahrain. He initiated the construction of the Bahrain International Circuit, and on April 4 2004 the Bahrain Grand Prix made history as the first Formula One Grand Prix to be held in the Middle East.

This would be the view one would have from the main grandstand. It is shaded from the blistering desert sun and there is a great view of the day's proceedings, in particular the start, as seen here in 2006.

The circuit was completed in 2004, ready for the first Middle East, FIA Formula One World Championship race. With a seating capacity of 50,000, and an overall weekend attendance estimated at around 100,000 people, this was going to be quite a spectacle.

A purpose-built media centre is capable of entertaining up to 500 journalists from around the world, and is equipped with all the latest in communication technology.

The circuit has numbers for its corners and the fastest sections are at the two ends of the two straights, which see a top speed of 320 kph being reached prior to turns 1 and 14. Turns 1 and 10 are the slowest corners, with a speed of only 80 kph.

In 2004 Michael Schumacher and the Ferrari team were still on a roll, and as predicted they finished in first place. The Ferrari covered the fifty-seven lap race in 1 hour, 28 minutes, 34.875 seconds, at an average speed of 209.143 kph. Schumacher also set the fastest lap of 1:30:252, creating an average speed of 216.074 kph.

A long view down the start straight, showing the procession of cars tucked up behind Felipe Massa and his Ferrari 248 F1. White smoke pours out from the side of his front tyre as he brakes hard to negotiate turn 1.

The Bahrain circuit boasts a state-of-the-art pit and paddock complex, which will accommodate up to eleven grand prix teams, their cars, all their equipment and their support staff. It lacks little and is a pleasant working environment.

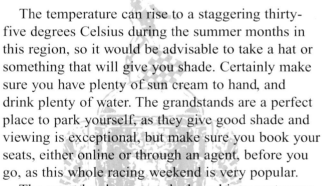

The temperature can rise to a staggering thirty-five degrees Celsius during the summer months in this region, so it would be advisable to take a hat or something that will give you shade. Certainly make sure you have plenty of sun cream to hand, and drink plenty of water. The grandstands are a perfect place to park yourself, as they give good shade and viewing is exceptional, but make sure you book your seats, either online or through an agent, before you go, as this whole racing weekend is very popular.

The event has been overshadowed in recent years due to protests from citizens of Bahrain who feel that the race should not take place. This is a result of the demonstrations and armed civil unrest that began in the country in 2011. That year, the Grand Prix was cancelled due to the ongoing violent demonstrations, and in subsequent years the situation in the country has been closely scrutinized before the races have been given the all clear.

It is hoped that the situation will find resolution soon so that competitors and race-goers alike can fully appreciate all that the circuit, the surrounding area and a peaceful Bahrain have to offer.

MALAYSIAN GRAND PRIX

Venue: Sepang International Circuit, Selangor, Malaysia

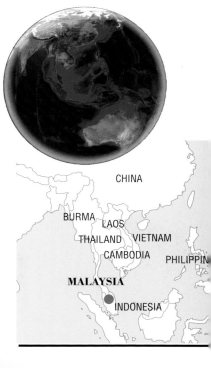

Sepang International Circuit was officially opened on 9 March 1999 by the Prime Minister Dato' Seri Dr Mahathir Mohamad, and was completed in a record fourteen months, receiving recognition for its ultra-modern facilities.

The circuit is situated 85 km from Kuala Lumpur city centre, and can be reached either by a modern North-South Expressway, railway links, or a network of highways. The circuit is located in the heart of the country's Multimedia Super Corridor, and is reached by air, rail and road. There are limousines, shuttle services and car rentals available at Kuala Lumpur International Airport (KLIA), which is only a ten-minute drive from the circuit. It is also served by major highways and expressways. From Kuala Lumpur (KL), take the North-South Highway towards the KLIA

Interchange: you should take roughly forty-five minutes to get to the circuit.

The Sepang F1 Circuit is a landmark for the fast-moving world of motorsport, setting standards of excellence as never before. The circuit was designed on 260 hectares of oil palm plantation, with some nine cubic metres of earth being removed, and the addition of 5,000 palm trees planted to help retain the natural beauty of the surrounding area.

Sepang International Circuit, Malaysia

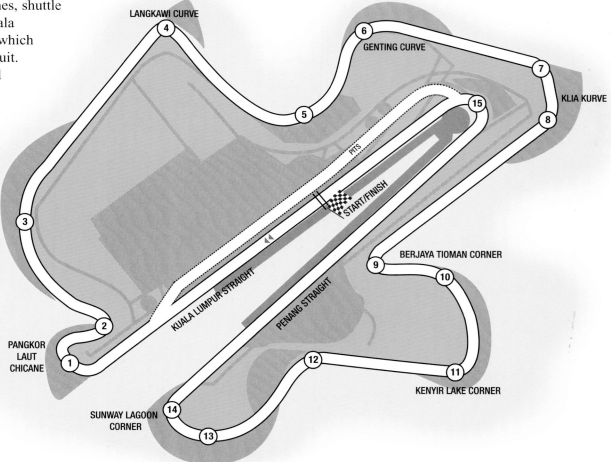

The circuit design is once again the work of the German architect Hermann Tilke and his company, who have also made huge contributions to other new and renovated circuits. The main circuit is generally raced in a clockwise direction, is 5.54 km long, and has fifteen corners and eight straights, with plenty of overtaking areas. The sweeping corners and wide straights are a main feature of the track, which has a very long back straight separated from the pit straight by just one very tight hairpin. A single lap distance on the Formula One circuit is 5.543 km (3.444 miles) long, and the race runs over fifty-six laps, for a total of 310.408 km (192.887 miles). Corners are numbered 1 to 15, with the fastest stretch being the

A scene shot during the 2006 Malaysian Grand Prix: Jenson Button in his Honda, surrounded by mechanics and technical staff prior to the start of the race. A tense moment for all involved.

pit straight, where the cars can reach a staggering 303 kph (190 mph). The slowest bend is right after the start at turn 1 and is taken at 85 kph (58 mph).

The circuit has been designed to be used for different types of racing and can be split using just certain parts of the track for particular events – there is a north side, 2.8 km long, and a south side, 2.6 km long, which can be used for different events at the same time. A special surface has been laid to cope with the Malaysian climate, made of specially formulated bitumen compound, making the surface smooth and not too abrasive. Probably the main attraction of the circuit is its pit building, which faces the main grandstand – this comprises thirty-three pit areas, the race control centre, time-keeping room, paddock clubs and race management offices.

A particularly good view of the Sepang circuit built and designed by Hermann Tilke and his design group. The large run-off areas are visible as are the sweeping, wide corners. Its facilities are also of the highest standard.

The start of the 2006 Malaysian Grand Prix: looking down the start/finish straight, Giancarlo Fisichella (Renault R26) leads Nico Rosberg (Williams FW28), Mark Webber (Williams FW28), Jenson Button (Honda RA106) and Fernando Alonso (Renault R26) in a rush towards turn 1 at Pangkor Laut chicane.

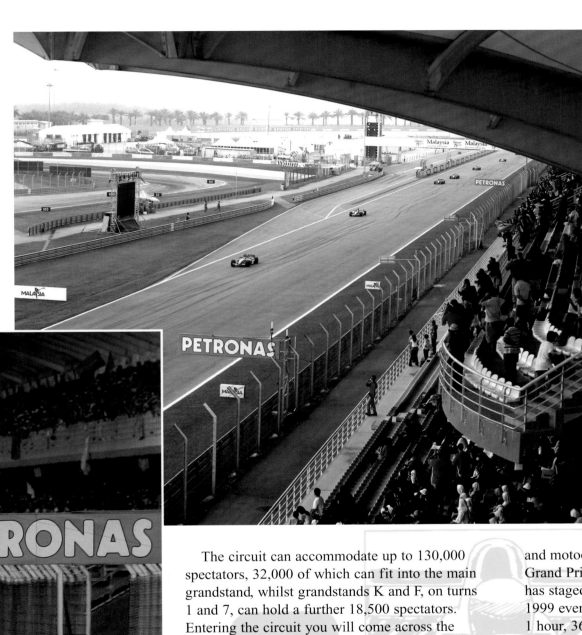

There can't be many better views than this one from the main grandstand: here, the two Renault R26s of Fisichella and Alonso are split by the Honda RA106 of Jenson Button as they stream past the grandstand at the start of another lap of the 2006 Grand Prix.

Sepang, March 19 2006: Jacques Villeneuve, in seventh position in his BMW Sauber F1.06, leads Fernando Alonso (Renault R26), who is in second position and seen in the distance. Some of the additional palm trees that have been planted can be spotted in the background.

The circuit can accommodate up to 130,000 spectators, 32,000 of which can fit into the main grandstand, whilst grandstands K and F, on turns 1 and 7, can hold a further 18,500 spectators. Entering the circuit you will come across the Welcome Centre, which houses the administration of the circuit and also houses a restaurant, the Sepang Circuit Shoppe and automotive museum. Safety, as can be imagined, is of prime importance, and Sepang has a dedicated medical centre, situated next to the pit building, which is transformed into a fully equipped mini-hospital during major events.

The Sepang Formula One International Circuit is the venue for the Malaysian Grand Prix, besides other motor racing events, and it also has kart racing and motocross facilities. The first Formula One Grand Prix took place at the circuit in 1999 and it has staged the race there ever since. The inaugural 1999 event was won by Eddie Irvine in a Ferrari in 1 hour, 36 minutes, 38.494 seconds. His team-mate, Michael Schumacher, followed him home just 0.01 seconds behind, and also posted the fastest lap in 1:40.267.

The brochure states: 'In the heart of Asia lie some of the most beautiful beaches in the world, with infinite carpets of sparkling white sand that stretch for miles and miles, and crystal-clear waters around exotic tropical islands.' This has to be enough to tempt most people, not only to the Grand Prix but to Malaysia too.

AUSTRALIAN GRAND PRIX

Venue: Albert Park, South Melbourne, Australia

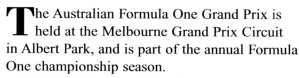

The Australian Formula One Grand Prix is held at the Melbourne Grand Prix Circuit in Albert Park, and is part of the annual Formula One championship season.

This has not always been the case, though, and as a non-world championship event, but still featuring Formula One cars, it has been held at various circuits around Australia, often attracting top drivers from around the world. The last such race was held in 1984.

It gained its status as part of the Formula One world championship in 1985, with the last race of the season held on the street circuit in Adelaide. The street circuit is a temporary track in the East Parklands, adjacent to the central business district of Adelaide in South Australia. It hosted a number of Grand Prix events from 1985 through to 1995, along with a series of special racing events, such as the Adelaide 500, a V8 Supercar race run on a shorter version of the Grand Prix track.

Although a tough street circuit, it was not as restrictive as Monaco and saw some great racing. For a street circuit it was quite quick and had long straights, with slow right-hand corners, but like other street circuits it didn't have much in the way of run-off areas. In fact the circuit was largely surrounded by large concrete walls, a hazard that none of the drivers were keen to mix with.

Tired of playing second fiddle to Sydney and Melbourne, Adelaide officials were determined to get this race event absolutely right and everybody

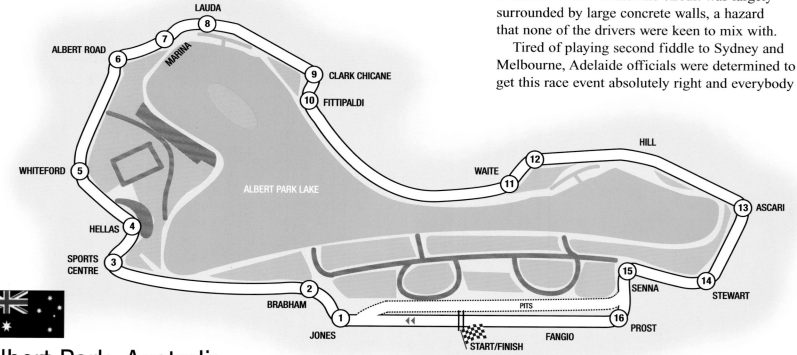

Albert Park, Australia

You could be forgiven for thinking this picture was taken at Monaco. In fact it is the Marina section of the Albert Park circuit, Melbourne, Australia. Shown here is Jacques Villeneuve driving a Williams FW18 Renault, in second position on his debut Grand Prix in 1996.

went to great lengths to do so. In fact the organization was so good that the teams voted it the best organized event in the calendar – repeating this on several other occasions too.

The first race was won by Keke Rosberg and also saw the final appearance of legendary race driver Niki Lauda. Probably the most memorable event came in 1986 when Nigel Mansell, Nelson Piquet and Alain Prost were still competing for the championship. Mansell only needed to finish third to guarantee the title, whilst Prost and Piquet needed not only to win, but for Mansell to finish lower than third to take the title. Disaster struck on the final laps of the race when Mansell, safely in the top three, picked up a puncture at very high speed,

RUNDLE ROAD / JONES STRAIGHT

MALTHOUSE CORNER

BRABHAM STRAIGHT / DEQUETTEVILLE TERRACE

HUTT STREET

FLINDERS STREET

EAST TERRACE

WAKEFIELD CORNER

WAKEFIELD ROAD

SENNA CHICANE

BRITANNIA ROUNDABOUT

RACE COURSE

START/FINISH

FOSTER'S CORNER

Adelaide, Australia

near the end of the main straight, creating a huge shower of sparks as the bottom of the vehicle grounded. Although Mansell fought to bring the car to a safe halt, his championship hopes had gone and Prost took the lead, won the race, and of course the championship.

Rain often disrupted the proceedings and during the 1989 event, after Prost had declined to continue after two laps, Thiery Boutsen scored a well-deserved win for the Williams team after most of the top drivers had all crashed or spun out. The 1991 race was even more of a disaster; this was stopped after only fourteen laps – making it the shortest Grand Prix ever – the race being won by Ayrton Senna.

The ultimate race on this circuit was staged in 1995 and won by Damon Hill, who finished two laps ahead of the rest of the field, including his team-mate Coulthard. The following year saw the race move to Melbourne.

Keke Rosberg in a Williams FW10 Honda, seen here in first position during the Australian Grand Prix at Adelaide in November 1985. In the background is the famous Stag Hotel, situated on Rundle Street. If you could get in, it was a great place to see the race.

Adelaide 1991: a wet Senna chicane leads on to Wakefield Road. Here, Nelson Piquet leads team-mate Michael Schumacher, both Benetton B191 Fords and both chased by Jean Alesi in a Ferrari 643 and Riccardo Patrese in a Williams FW14 Renault at the start.

central Melbourne, and the track uses everyday sections of road around Albert Park's man-made lake. With the road sections being rebuilt to make sure they were smooth and up to standard for the race cars, it is an attractive circuit with great facilities and picturesque scenery.

The circuit comes to life about four weeks prior to the race, when workmen start to erect all the barriers, grandstands, overpasses and other sections of the motorsport infrastructure. These are eventually removed within two weeks of the end of the race and so disruption to the park is minimal – although local residents still make their complaints heard. Nevertheless, the week's events are very popular in Melbourne and the rest of Australia, not to mention with the other fanatics who travel the thousands of miles to attend.

The circuit uses numbers, not names, for its corners, but has given its strategically placed stands names after great racing drivers. Following the track

It was 1993 when well-known businessman Ron Walker commenced negotiations to bring the Grand Prix to Melbourne. Later that year it was announced that the event would be held at a rebuilt Albert Park street circuit in Melbourne, which it was in 1996. It wasn't a straightforward affair though, with protesters from the 'Save Albert Park' group doing everything they could to disrupt the move. Albert Park is a fashionable suburb of Melbourne and is characterized by wide leafy streets with open-air cafes, delicatessens and boutiques. Although the race circuit required trees to be cut down and facilities demolished, funds were injected for replacement facilities. The lake circuit is popular with strollers, runners and cyclists, whilst dozens of small yachts sail around the lake on sunny days. It's also the birthplace of Australian football legend Roy Cazaly.

The Melbourne Grand Prix Circuit is a street-based circuit only a couple of kilometres south of from the start/finish line you accelerate along the first straight reaching about 310 kph before negotiating both the Jones and Brabham stands – corners 1 and 2. Hard on the accelerator out of these corners and up to 295 kph before negotiating corner 3, at about 76 kph, and corner 4, at 144 kph. Pulling away swiftly you will then take the slight right-hander at Whiteford, at around 230 kph, and onwards to Albert Park Road – turn 6 – reaching about 285 kph, before braking for the corner. Now onwards still through turns 7 and 8, reaching Clark at a staggering 288 kph. Through 9 and 10 and onwards to 11, where you will again reach a speed

With a great backdrop of Melbourne city centre, seen here at the 2006 Australian Grand Prix at Albert Park is Ralf Schumacher in a Toyota TF106. He finished in third position.

Pictured during the 1990 Australian Grand Prix in Adelaide, Ayrton Senna (McLaren MP4/5B Honda) leads Thierry Boutsen (Williams FW13B Renault). In the background is the well-known John Martin's Department Store on Rundle Street.

A shot taken at the 1994 Australian Grand Prix in Adelaide, showing the streets and buildings of the city in the background and Gerhard Berger in his Ferrari 412T1B in second position in the foreground.

of 288 kph. Corners 11 and 12 will be taken at around 212 kph and 216 kph, rocketing back up to 287 kph at Hill, then touching 298 kph before negotiating Ascari – corner 13 – at 122 kph. Corner 14 is Stewart and taken at 165 kph before a sharp left, 75 kph, which takes you to Prost. This is corner 16 and the last, so accelerate hard, through the start/finish line and onwards again to Jones, reaching some 310 kph. Only 57 more laps to complete, giving a race distance of about 307 km with a circuit length of 5.3 km.

Although the spectators are well fenced in around the circuit, there have to be openings in the fences for the marshals to be able to get on to the track. Disaster struck in 2001, when a flying tyre from

a crashed car hit a volunteer track marshal and fatally injured him.

The following year, though, there was great excitement when Australian driver Mark Webber, who was at the time driving a very uncompetitive Minardi, finished in fifth position. This threw the whole of Australia into frenzy mode, and Michael Schumacher, who won the race, was relegated to minor celebrity status. In 2008, rookie Lewis Hamilton started his bid for what would become his first World Championship, with a superior drive to win the race for McLaren.

Large scale changes to the rules for the 2009 championship resulted in teams struggling at the start of the season to make their cars competitive. Honda had pulled out of racing and the team was taken over by the Brawn organization, headed up by Ross Brawn and with sponsorship from Virgin.

The drivers remained the same – Jenson Button and Rubens Barrichello. It was a surprise to everybody when Button secured pole position but as Button himself commented, it was like a dream come true when he won the race. The icing on the cake was seeing Barrichello come in second place making a Brawn one-two on their first outing. Honda must have been kicking themselves.

Jenson Button, Brawn GP BGP001, leads team mate Rubens Barrichello across the line to a one-two victory in the Australian Grand Prix at the Albert Park circuit, Melbourne on 29 March 2009.

SAN MARINO GRAND PRIX

Venue: Autodromo Enzo e Dino Ferrari, Imola, Bologna, Italy

According to legend, Marino left the island of Rab with his lifelong friend Leo and went to the town of Rimini as a stone worker. After persecution because of his Christian sermons, he escaped to the nearby Mt Titano, where he built a small church and thus founded what is now the city and the state of San Marino. The official date of foundation of the republic is 3 September 301 AD.

San Marino, a little like Monaco, is a separate principality but located within Italy. It is divided into nine municipalities, known locally as castles, of which the City of San Marino (Città di San Marino) is the eponymous capital. The town of Imola, located in the province of Bologna, in the Emilia-Romagna region of north-central Italy, is the home of the Autodromo Enzo e Dino Ferrari and the San Marino Formula One Grand Prix. The race was named after

Autodromo Enzo e Dino Ferrari, Italy

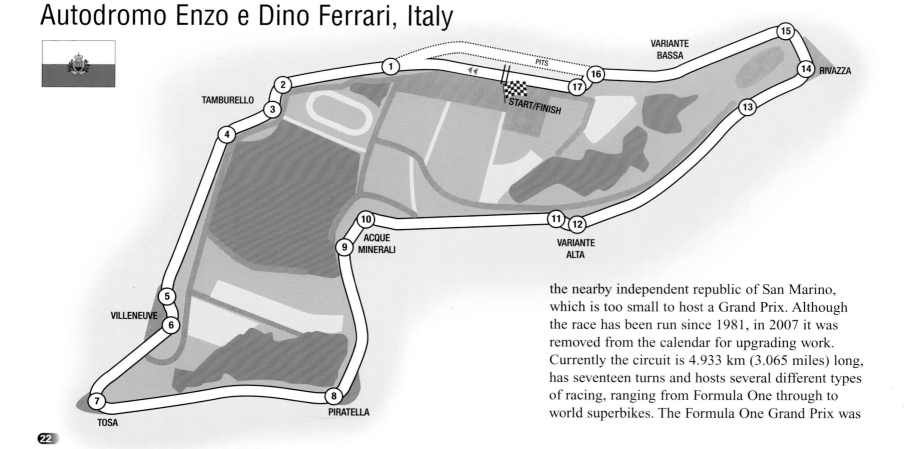

the nearby independent republic of San Marino, which is too small to host a Grand Prix. Although the race has been run since 1981, in 2007 it was removed from the calendar for upgrading work. Currently the circuit is 4.933 km (3.065 miles) long, has seventeen turns and hosts several different types of racing, ranging from Formula One through to world superbikes. The Formula One Grand Prix was

A scene from the 2006 San Marino Grand Prix at Imola, with Michael Schumacher (Ferrari 248F1) in first position leading Jenson Button (Honda RA106) in seventh position, as they come out of Tosa and head uphill for Piratella. Felipe Massa in the other Ferrari is fourth and Fernando Alonso (Renault R26) is in second position.

generally sixty-two laps long, covering a distance of 305,846 km (190,044 miles).

The area around Imola is the home of several well-known Italian sports car manufacturers – Ferrari, Lamborghini and Maserati, to name three. It was after the Second World War that four local motor racing enthusiasts proposed the construction of a new road linking existing public roads, which could be used by the local car manufacturers to test their prototypes. Construction began in March 1950, and the first test run took place two years later when Enzo Ferrari sent a car to the track. In 1953 the first

On April 21 1963, an unofficial Formula One race was run at Imola. Although of minor importance, a young driver, Jim Clark, won the race with his Lotus. Clark would go on to become one of the most respected drivers of his time, his life cut short when he was killed during a minor Formula 2 race at the Hockenheimring on April 7 1968.

Built in 1950 by a group of motoring enthusiasts, the Imola race track was simply a collection of new roads joining existing public highways, which consisted of the area enclosed between the right bank of the Santerno River, the Acqua Minerale Park and the foot of the Santerno hills, seen here.

motorcycle race took place and a year later the first car race was held.

Jim Clark, in a Lotus, won the first non-championship Formula One race, held in July 1963. Soon after this, the council in Imola decided to name the circuit after Enzo Ferrari's son Dino, who had tragically died in 1956. This move created a strong bond with Enzo Ferrari, whilst also helping to raise enough capital to make the track into a permanent, closed circuit. After Enzo died in August 1988, the

The sign posting to the Imola circuit is excellent. This sign shows the way to the well-known Tosa corner. The circuit is in the Acque Minerali Park, just outside the town of Imola itself.

to the circuit to see their current Ferrari hero. In 1981 Gilles Villeneuve, father of the current Jacques, crashed his Ferrari at the corner which today bears his name. The following year he returned, even more determined to win the race. A real battle ensued with his then team-mate Didier Pironi, who snatched a slim victory. Villeneuve was incensed, stating that Pironi had disobeyed team orders, and then vowed he would never speak to him again. Sadly he didn't have to keep his promise for very long as at the next race at Zolder, he was killed in a horrific accident during the practice session.

name was changed again to Autodromo Enzo e Dino Ferrari, in honour of these two great people.

In 1979 Niki Lauda, in a Brabham-Alfa Romeo, won a second non-championship Formula One race.

Monza is a legendary circuit in Italy, and the home of the Italian Grand Prix. Back in 1978, there was a devastating start-line pile-up at Monza, in which the popular Swedish driver Ronnie Peterson was killed. As a direct result of this event, the race was moved to Imola for 1980, and so the first official Formula One race was held there as the 51st Italian Grand Prix. Then in the following year, the first official San Marino Grand Prix was held at the Imola circuit, and the Italian Grand Prix returned to its home venue of Monza. The race was won by Nelson Piquet in a Brabham BT49C, in 1 hour, 51 minutes, 23.970 seconds. He was followed in by Riccardo Patrese in an Arrows A3, and Carlos Reutemann came third in a Williams FW07C.

During the following years races came and went, but because of its proximity to the Ferrari factory, Imola has always had a unique atmosphere. For the 'Tifosi' this weekend is like a pilgrimage to a religious shrine, and every year they travel en masse

In 1980 the Italian Formula One Grand Prix was held at Imola whilst major work was done at Monza. The first official San Marino Formula One Grand Prix was held at Imola in 1981. Seen here is the winner of that race, Nelson Piquet, in his Brabham BT49C Ford.

As a tribute to Villeneuve, Patrick Tambay, racing a Ferrari the following year, donned the number 27 and took the Ferrari to victory. He said later that the car seemed to do things he was not asking it to do, and went on to say that it was as if Gilles had been in the car with him. It was without doubt an unlikely outcome, but one that will go down in motor racing history for more reasons than one.

More accidents happened in the following years with Nelson Piquet and Gerhard Berger narrowly escaping death, during accidents at the very fast Tamburello corner. In 1994, though, things seemed to go from bad to worse. It was without doubt one of the saddest weekends in motor racing history. During Friday morning, Rubens Barrichello crashed and was knocked unconscious at the Variante Bassa. As if that wasn't bad enough, Roland Ratzenberger was tragically killed on the Saturday at the Villeneuve corner, with just minutes of qualifying left. Nobody believed it could get any worse, but it did! As the race started to settle, the car of racing legend Ayrton Senna was seen going straight on at the Tamburello corner. His Williams FW16 was travelling at 192 mph (309 kph), when it ran wide at a curve and crashed into a concrete wall. The front right tyre and suspension, detached by the impact, hit Senna on the head and pierced his visor, causing the fatal trauma. The race was red-flagged and Senna was airlifted to Maggiore Hospital, where he died several hours later.

These were the darkest and most depressing days for motor racing, when safety was not what it is today, and drivers were truly in the greatest danger if they crashed. But lessons were learned from these

A photo of the 2001 San Marino Grand Prix. It is easy to see why the drivers love this circuit. Wide track and good run-off areas in addition to wonderful backgrounds make Imola very attractive.

Probably one of the darkest moments in motor racing history was the 1994 San Marino Grand Prix. Ayrton Senna (Williams FW16 Renault) is seen here leading Michael Schumacher (Benetton B194 Ford). It was during this race that Senna crashed heavily and lost his life.

tragedies and as well as the Tamburello corner being changed into a chicane, many more changes took place at other circuits and in the sport generally to make it safer. It isn't all gloom and doom though and Imola has also seen some of the most exciting and best racing over the years it has been operating.

The San Marino Grand Prix was put in doubt when it was left off the calendar for 2007. Refurbishment was needed and did take place, but it has yet to reappear as part of the championship season. The circuit, as a Formula One venue is now surely in doubt, even though other racing will continue to take place. Imola is very accessible as a circuit. It is just 30 km from t.he beautiful city of Bologna and its international airport of Guglielmo Marconi. Airlines fly there from many of the European countries along with long-haul flights too. Bologna is a place that must be visited, nestling in the rolling hills of the Emilia-Romagna countryside. It is also the headquarters of the 'slow food movement', an international organization dedicated to eating and drinking in the most relaxed way possible. There is no doubt that the local food in this area is a little special, and it should be savoured in a relaxing environment, of which there are plenty.

It was scenes like this that worried the organizers at Imola and the reason for the circuit being omitted from the Formula One race calendar in 2007. Fans streaming on to the circuit, on occasions even when the race was not finished, created a dangerous situation for both fans and drivers.

You can travel to the circuit by car, taking the motorway (autostrada), and there are plenty of parking spaces when you get there. Bologna is a major train station with a connection to Imola, via the Bologna to Ancona line. A short walk at the other end will bring you to the main entrance of the circuit.

For those real Ferrari enthusiasts, the sacred temple of Ferrari is situated about forty-five minutes' drive away at Maranello. Here you will be able to wander around in amazement in the museum, which is stacked full of historical information as well as the latest cars. Visit the Fiorano test track, which is nearby, and watch as the cars come and go from the factory.

As far as the weather is concerned, be careful and take protection from very hot spring sunshine. It can get excessively hot around the circuit. On the other hand it has also been known to snow at this time of the year too, so be prepared and look at the weather forecast before you set off!

SINGAPORE GRAND PRIX

Venue: Marina Bay Street Circuit, Singapore

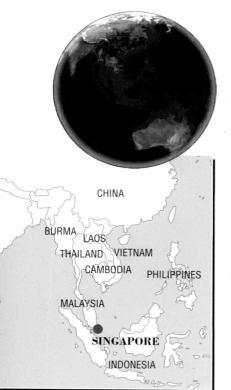

The 2008 Singapore Grand Prix was the first Formula One race to be run in Singapore, and the first to take place at night. The cars run in an anti-clockwise direction on this 5.067 km (3.148 mile) street circuit, which also enhances safety.

The new street circuit, which has a total of 23 turns, offers a number of overtaking opportunities, with challenging corners and gruelling sections capable of testing the best Formula One driver. Although originally designed by Herman Tilke, the circuit has since changed slightly. Originally organized in 1961, the race was then known as the

Singapore Grand Prix. In 1962 it was renamed the Malaysian Grand Prix and remained one of Singapore's major sporting attractions. A further name-change to the Singapore Grand Prix came in 1965 after Singapore attained its independence. The event continued to be run up to 1973, after which it was discontinued for a variety of reasons, including an increase in traffic and several fatal accidents. The last person to win the Singapore Grand Prix was Vern Schuppan in 1973, when the venue was known as the Thomson Road Grand Prix circuit.

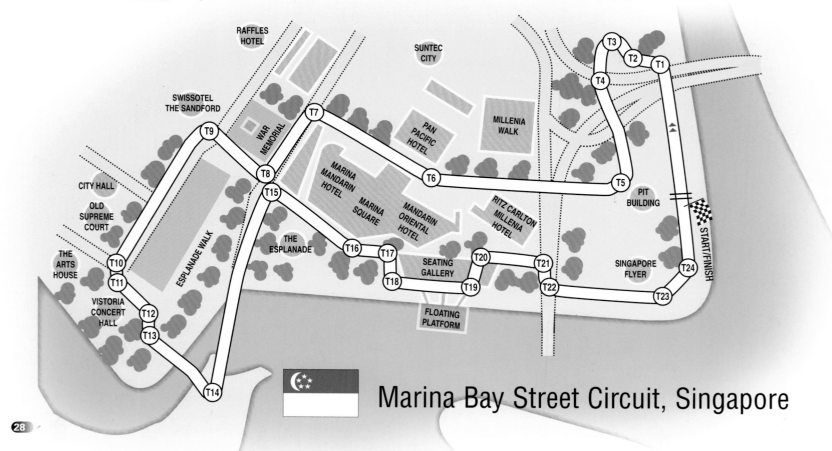

Marina Bay Street Circuit, Singapore

Eagerly awaited by fans from around the world, the new 2008 Singapore Formula One Grand Prix lacked nothing. Exotic venue, exciting racing by floodlight, lots of overtaking and a surprise win for Fernando Alonso – his first win since Monza 2007. The first race was a great success, and subsequent events have ensured Singapore is contracted to remain on the calendar until at least 2017.

Fernando Alonso in his Renault R28, patiently counts down the laps to bring his car in just ahead of Nico Rosberg and win the race.

Heikki Kovalainen, McLaren MP4-23 Mercedes, pits for refuelling. He finished 10th after being involved in a first-lap skirmish with Kubica.

SPANISH GRAND PRIX

Venue: Circuit de Catalunya, Montmeló, Barcelona, Spain

The Spanish Formula One Grand Prix currently alternates each year between the Circuit de Catalunya in Barcelona and the Valencia Street Circuit around Valencia's harbour, which hosted the European Grand Prix from 2008 until 2012.

Circuit de Catalunya is situated in Montmeló, north of Barcelona, and has long straights and a good variety of corners. It is seen as an all-rounder circuit ideal for testing, which several of the teams take advantage of during the pre-season period and even during the season itself. There is not a great deal of opportunity for overtaking and the circuit has a reputation for being a little bland, but it has also seen some thrilling racing over the years. It was inaugurated in 1991 and consists of three different routes: the Grand Prix track, 4.730 km in length,

the National track, 3.067 km and the School track, 1.703 km long. The Formula One race distance is 307.323 km over a total of sixty-five laps. It was on 3 October 1986 that the Catalan Parliament unanimously approved a green paper requesting the Executive Council to 'co-ordinate the relevant bodies in order to conduct a study and join forces to create a new permanent racing circuit'. On 24 February 1989 the Circuit Consortium was established between the Generalitat, the Town Council of Montmeló and the RACC, and the agreement with the Consejo Superior de Deportes (CSD) was signed. That very day the first stone was laid for the Circuit de Catalunya. The official opening took place on 10 September 1991, and just five days later the circuit hosted its first official

Circuit de Catalunya, Spain

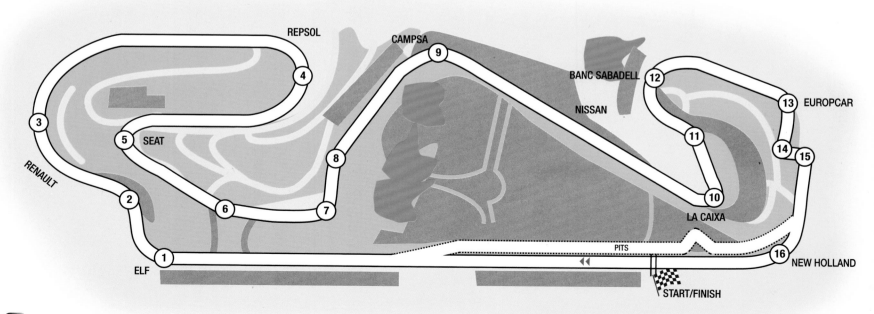

A familiar sight is the Tilke-designed grandstand, seen here during the start of the 2006 Spanish Grand Prix at the Circuit de Catalunya, Barcelona. Reigning World Champion Fernando Alonso in a Renault R26 leads his team-mate Giancarlo Fisichella in the other Renault, as the pack stream down towards the Elf corner at the start of the sixty-six lap race.

race, the Spanish Touring Car Championship, won by ex-Formula One driver Luis Pérez Sala. On 29 September 1991, the 35th Formula One Spanish Grand Prix took place, sixteen years after it was held in Catalonia for the last time.

Although motor racing events had taken place in Spain prior to 1913, the first Spanish Grand Prix was run in that year. It was run to touring car rules rather than the traditional Grand Prix formula known at the time. The venue was a 300 km road circuit at Guadarrama, near Madrid, and the winner was Carlos de Salamanca in a Rolls Royce. The best-known race prior to this was the Catalan Cup, which took place in 1908 and 1909. The route was arranged around the city of Sitges, near Barcelona, and both races were won by Jules Goux. Following these races a permanent, oval circuit was built at Sitges in 1922 and known as Sitges-Terramar. The new circuit was 2 km in length, varied in width and had banking on the corners. The 1923 Spanish Grand Prix was held here and won by Albert Divo

The Rolls Royce Silver Ghost earned its reputation for durability, economy and reliability in very early competitions, particularly in long-distance trials. It took first place in the 1913 Spanish Touring Car Grand Prix in the hands of Rolls Royce's Spanish agent, Don Carlos de Salamanca. He is seen here with his mechanic on his way to victory on the Guadarrama circuit.

The 1926 European Grand Prix took place at the Lasarte circuit, San Sebastian, on July 18 1926. The five-and-a-half hour race was won by Meo Costantini in a Bugatti T39A. Here he is seen taking a pit stop, which in those days was a bit less hectic than today!

in a Sunbeam, but with financial problems and the distance from Barcelona also a problem, the circuit ran into difficulties. By 1925 the circuit was virtually abandoned until Edgard de Morawitz purchased it in the 1930s. The 1932 Spanish Motorcycle Grand Prix was held there along with one or two other races, but not long after these events the circuit was once again abandoned.

This didn't signal the end of motor racing in Spain, and the 1926 Grand Prix of Europe was held at yet another circuit. The Circuito Lasarte, just over eleven miles long, was located in the Basque region, near the resort of San Sebastian on the Bay of

Biscay. The 1926 race was won by Meo Constantini in a Bugatti. The circuit hosted the Grand Prix, on and off, up to 1935, when the Spanish Civil War erupted. With Spain descending into civil war, to be followed shortly by the Second World War, motor racing was not the most important thing on people's minds, and this would remain the case until after the conflicts.

The first race to take place on Spanish soil after 1945 was the Penya Rhin Grand Prix, which took place on the roads of Barcelona on the Pedralbes circuit. Although that was not an official Formula One race, in 1951 the Grand Prix circus returned to Spain, and a fierce battle of the racing kind took place at the Pedralbes circuit between Juan Manual Fangio and Alberto Ascari. This was the last race of the season and either driver could clinch the championship, which ended up going to the legendary Fangio in his Alfa Romeo. It would be a further three years before another Grand Prix would be held in Spain, and again it was at the Pedralbes

First opened in 1946 in the western suburbs of Barcelona, Pedralbes featured wide streets and expansive, sweeping corners, and was loved by both drivers and racing fans. Here a cameraman takes the opportunity to get some close-up action of the great Juan Manuel Fangio, winner of the 1951 race in his Alfa Romeo 159.

Although an unofficial Grand Prix was held at the Jarama circuit in 1967, the official Spanish Grand Prix was held there in May 1968. Chris Amon, in a Ferrari 312 and in pole position, is seen being left behind by Pedro Rodriguez in a BRM P133. Denny Hulme in a McLaren M7A Ford makes a good start on the outside too. The race was won by Graham Hill in a Lotus-Cosworth.

circuit: this time the race was won by Mike Hawthorn in a Ferrari.

In 1955 a terrible accident happened at the Le Mans circuit, where seventy-seven people were killed when two cars collided on the race track and crashed into the spectators' stand. This prompted new regulations regarding crowds, and as a result the spectator-lined Pedralbes circuit became a victim of the situation, never to be used again for Grand Prix racing.

Once again the Spanish Grand Prix disappeared from the calendar and would not be seen again until the 1960s, when the Royal Automobile Club of Spain organized the building of the Jarama circuit, north of Madrid. At the same time another, older circuit in Barcelona was also resurrected; this was known as the Montjuic Park circuit. From nothing, suddenly Spain had two circuits!

Jarama hosted a non-championship race in 1967, which was won by Jim Clark, and the following year the official Grand Prix returned to the circuit. The race was won by Graham Hill in a Lotus, a fitting tribute to Jim Clark, who had lost his life just a few weeks before. From here onwards the race alternated between Montjuic Park and Jarama for the next few years. The end of racing at Montjuic Park came in 1975, when drivers complained about the circuit not

The 1969 Spanish Grand Prix took place at the Monjuich Park circuit, Barcelona, and was won by Jackie Stewart. The wing on the back of his Matra MS80 Ford was used to help keep the rear of the car on the ground.

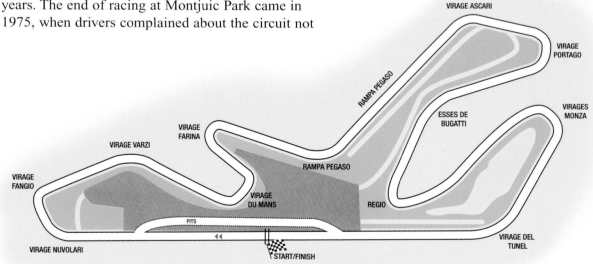

Circuito Permanente del Jarama, Spain

being safe, Emmerson Fittipaldi even retiring in protest. In fact disaster struck on the 26th lap when Rolf Stommelen's car crashed and killed four people. From here onwards Jarama hosted races up to 1981, after which it too was dropped from the racing calendar.

Again, this was not the end of racing in Spain and the Grand Prix returned in 1985 at yet another new circuit. This time the Mayor of Jerez, keen to promote the town and its sherries, backed a project to build a new circuit: Formula One had returned! The Circuito Permanente de Jerez was ready for the 1986 season and it couldn't have been a more thrilling race. It was a classic duel between Nigel Mansell and Ayrton Senna, with the race being

decided on the line as the two crossed neck and neck. Senna claimed the glory, beating Mansell by a mere 0.014 seconds.

Jerez never captured the hearts of the nation and spectators never came in large numbers, so 1990 saw the last official Formula One Grand Prix at the circuit. The new Circuit de Catalunya was ready for the 1991 Formula One Grand Prix, and there it has stayed ever since. The first race was won by Nigel Mansell in a Williams-Renault, followed in second place by Alain Prost in a Ferrari.

The circuit is situated near the city of Barcelona, which has a Mediterranean climate of mild winters and hot, dry summers. Although the Grand Prix is held at the beginning of the year, it can still be very hot at that time of the season, and so some precautions should be taken. Although viewing is pretty good from all of the stands, it is worth keeping in mind that Elf corner is one of the track's few overtaking opportunities and therefore a good place to park yourself – keep in mind you will not be the only one there! In 2007 there was a record

The huge scoreboard positioned just at the exit to the pit lane of the Catalunya circuit denotes that Fernando Alonso, driving a Renault R26, car number one, is leading the 2006 Spanish Grand Prix on lap nineteen.

The dramatic scene at the end of the 1986 Spanish Grand Prix at the Jerez circuit: the photo shows Ayrton Senna, driving a Lotus 98T Renault, crossing the line 14/100ths of a second ahead of Nigel Mansell, driving a Williams FW11 Honda, to win the race. This was one of the closest finishes in Grand Prix history.

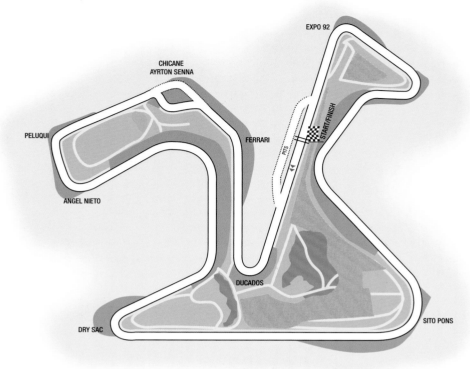

EXPO 92

CHICANE
AYRTON SENNA

PELUQUI

FERRARI

PITS

START/FINISH

ANGEL NIETO

DUCADOS

DRY SAC

SITO PONS

Circuito Permanente de Jerez, Spain

The Circuit de Catalunya near Barcelona is a popular Grand Prix venue as can be seen by the crowds in the background. Here, Tiago Monteiro in a Midland M16-Toyota leads his team-mate Christijan Albers in the other Midland M16-Toyota.

The 2004 Spanish Grand Prix: Olivier Panis in his Toyota TF104 has pulled into the pits for refuelling and tyre change. These pit stops take a matter of seconds and are carried out with military precision, as they can determine the outcome of a race.

140,000 people at the Grand Prix, many of whom were there for their local hero Fernando Alonso. Although numbers have declined to around 90,000 in 2012, it's worth making sure you have tickets before you get there. The circuit offers good amenities and can be easily reached from Barcelona by car or train (there is a short walk from Montmelo Station). The nearest international airport is El Prat de Llobragat in Barcelona, which is just 47 km from the circuit.

For 2008 the European Formula One Grand Prix changed venues from Germany to Spain; a new circuit was created around the streets of Valencia, incorporating the port area. The new 5.5 km (3.5 mile) circuit, with its twisty street sections and beautiful harbour location, has offered exciting racing and typical Mediterranean cool for its spectators. Felipe Massa pipped Lewis Hamilton to pole position for the first race and kept his nerve to drive to victory in his 100th Grand Prix.

The blur that is Felipe Massa, seen in his Ferrari F2008, on his way to winning the very first European Grand Prix held at the all new Valencia circuit in Spain. The street circuit will alternately host the Spanish Grand Prix with the Circuit de Catalunya from 2013.

Valencia Street Circuit, Spain

PUERTO AUTÓNOMO DE VALENCIA

MONACO GRAND PRIX

Venue: Circuit de Monaco, Monte Carlo, Monaco

The Monaco Grand Prix is one of the oldest of the Formula One race events to remain on the calendar. It also rates as the most thrilling and eventful, both on and off the track, the race being run literally on the streets of Monte Carlo. It is without doubt spectacular in every respect, with visitors flying, driving and sailing in from around the world and from all walks of life. From princesses to backpackers, they all come to enjoy the spectacle, buzz and glitz that takes the place over, and at one of the most striking and colourful venues in the world.

Although probably the most dangerous of all the tracks, it is still a favourite and people flock every year to grab a space somewhere around this tight twisty street circuit. The streets are cordoned off by railings and barriers and the whole area becomes engulfed in a Formula One frenzy. Hotels are booked years ahead and unless you have booked in advance, there is no chance of staying in the city and very little chance you will find anywhere decent nearby. Hotels can be booked that are situated right on the circuit, so viewing is not only better than in front of a television, you can also become totally engulfed in all the build-up and razzmatazz of the three-day event.

Anthony Noghes, who was president of the Monegasque car club and close friend

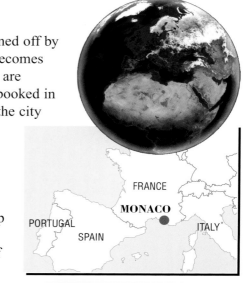

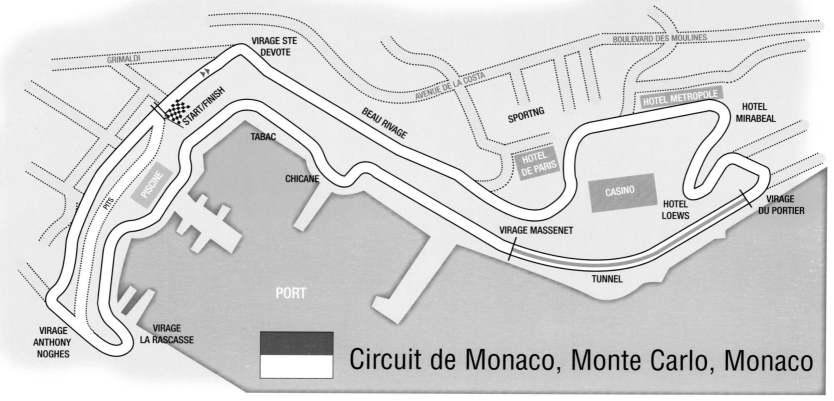

Circuit de Monaco, Monte Carlo, Monaco

An incredible bird's eye view of the Monaco circuit: the sharp left-hander to the right of the building is Lowes, and Kimi Raikkonen can be seen in his McLaren Mercedes MP4-20 leading the field under the flyover, heading to the Virage du Portier, which in turn leads to the tunnel. This is the start of the 2005 Grand Prix.

of the ruling Grimaldi family, hatched the idea to have a race around the streets of Monaco. He consulted with race driver of the period Louis Chiron, and with his approval and help he staged the inaugural race in 1929. Chiron unfortunately did not attend the race as he was due to enter the Indy 500, which was run on the same weekend. As it was, the race was won by William Grover-Williams, a racing driver and war hero born to an English father and a French mother in the Montrouge suburb of Paris, France. He drove a Bugatti type 35B, painted in what would become known as British racing green. He beat the heavily favoured Mercedes car driven by the notorious German driver, Rudolf Caracciola.

Just to put things into perspective, the Bugatti covered the 100 lap race in 3 hours, 56 minutes and

A photo taken during the Thursday practice session for the 2006 Monaco Grand Prix: this is the 'Piscine' (swimming pool) section, with Tabac directly below on the right. The whole Port area is buzzing during the Grand Prix, with people mooring their mega-expensive boats as near to the track as possible. Cocktail time seems to be never-ending!

Felipe Massa guides his Ferrari 248F1 through the deposits of rubber that have been shed during the race. The racing line can easily be seen here, and moving away from it can be treacherous, especially if you end up going over the rubber particles. This picture was taken during the 2006 Monaco Grand Prix.

A scene from the Monaco Grand Prix of 1929. It makes a stark difference from the race we see today: tramlines, no crash barriers, lampposts and smartly dressed people were the order of the day. The drivers even had time to wave to the spectators! Here, 'W Williams' (real name William Grover-Williams) guides his Bugatti T35B past the start/finish line to take first place.

11 seconds – attaining an average speed of 80.194 kph. In 2005, Kimi Raikkonen in his McLaren Mercedes completed the 78 lap race in 1 hour, 45 minutes and 15 seconds – attaining an average speed of 148.501 kph. How life moves on!

Juan Manuel Fangio won the first Monaco Grand Prix to count towards the F1 World Championship; however it would be 1955 before the Monaco Grand Prix would be a regular occurrence on the Formula One calendar. Since then the race has been won by legends such as Stirling Moss, Graham Hill – once nicknamed 'Mister Monaco' because of his five overall wins – Gilles Villeneuve, Alain Prost, Ayrton Senna – who overtook the great Graham Hill and scored an unsurpassed six wins – and Michael Schumacher, to name a few.

Although there is little overtaking, due to the tight streets and sharp bends, many drivers try hard to get past their challengers with heart-stopping manoeuvres that thrill and excite the hordes of cheering spectators. Some do come to grief but others seem to make a habit of scrabbling past – and as calmly as you like. There have been several accidents at the circuit, with drivers even ending up in the harbour water (though most have escaped injury). The most tragic though was probably the fatal accident of Lorenzo Bandini in 1967 when in May of that year, running second to Denny Hulme, he lost control of his car at the harbour chicane and crashed. The car rolled over and caught fire, with Bandini trapped beneath it. He was rushed to the local hospital but his burns were so terrible that three days later he died of his injuries.

The noise too is exceptional, and although it makes the adrenalin pump harder, the eardrums do take a bashing. Earplugs are a recommendation as the noise can be earth shattering as it rebounds around the buildings.

The tunnel probably has to be the most daunting part of the circuit to the driver, particularly on a

Graham Hill, easily recognized by his black helmet with small strips, was a master of the Monaco circuit and won it on five occasions – the 1968 race being no exception. Here Hill, driving a Lotus 49B-Ford, is hounded by Jo Siffert, also in a Lotus. Siffert unfortunately had to retire due to differential problems.

Juan Manuel Fangio is seen fighting his Alfa Romeo 158 around the Port area during the Monaco Grand Prix of 1950, in which he finished first. This whole area was changed on several occasions before it ended up looking like it does today, replete with luxury yachts and beautiful people.

bright day. The move is suddenly from light to dark, with barely enough time for the eyes to get used to the dark, and the drivers are then thrust out into the bright sunlight again. It plays havoc with eyesight and judgement, especially when you imagine that they are reaching speeds in excess of 270 kph.

Minor adjustments were made to the layout over the early years, but initially the circuit itself remained free of major work and its length was unchanged at 3,180 metres right up to 1950. In 1952 some modifications were made to the Saint Dévote bend, which resulted in the shortening of the track to 3,145 metres. Then in 1973 the layout was changed again and the circuit this time was extended a

The Monaco Grand Prix of 1967: Chris Amon in a Ferrari 312 passes the wreckage of team-mate Lorenzo Bandini. Bandini was in second position when he lost control of his car at the harbour chicane. The car hit the wall, rolled over and burst into flames, leaving him trapped. Although marshals managed to flip his car upright and pull him out, he suffered major burns and died in hospital three days later.

The tunnel at Monaco is quite well lit but when you're travelling at excessively high speeds and move from light to semi-dark and back to light again in a matter of seconds, it can be confusing. Here Mika Hakkinen (McLaren MP4/13 Mercedes-Benz) emerges from the tunnel during practice for the 1998 Monaco Grand Prix.

further 135 metres with the addition of a new piece along the port area. This joined the track around the new pool and ended in a hairpin bend around the 'La Rascasse' restaurant. Following this adjustment, grandstands were reinstalled on the old quay. As the

This picture was taken just after the start of the 1996 Monaco Grand Prix. Drivers have to keep their nerve as wheels intertwine, leaving them just millimetres away from chaos. Eddie Irvine (Ferrari F310) negotiates Ste. Devote, with Rubens Barrichello (Jordan 196 Peugeot) going through on the inside while David Coulthard (McLaren MP4/11B Mercedes) follows.

length of each lap increased, so the Grand Prix was shortened to seventy-eight laps. In 1976, the addition of a further two chicanes – one at Sainte Dévote and the other coming round the La Rascasse hairpin bend – extended the length by thirty-four metres.

Further adjustments took place in 1986 with the widening of the Quai des Etats-Unis and the addition of a new chicane. Then in 1997 the original S-bend around the swimming pool was redesigned and named after the local French driver who was

instrumental in starting the whole thing off – Louis Chiron. In 2003, 5,000 square metres of land was reclaimed from the sea and the circuit between the second S-bend of the swimming pool and the Rascasse was moved ten metres and completely redesigned. For 2004, work doubled the width of the promenade, where the pits on the boulevard Albert 1st are located, by building over the old track between the swimming pool and the Rascasse. A further 250 square metres of new pit area was provided for the teams.

The circuit has several very famous landmarks. The Grand Prix begins with a short burst of heavy acceleration before the perilous right-hand Virage St Dévote is encountered. This is a bottleneck and many an accident is bound to happen here. The speeds that are attained from the start line are phenomenal, but in a very short time they reach the bend and everybody is stamping hard on the brakes, which inevitably causes a concertina-type situation. Jostling for position, drivers are desperate to avoid

For anybody who has been to Monaco, at Grand Prix time or not, this is a familiar sight. Michael Schumacher, driving a Benetton B194 Ford, negotiates Casino Square in first position. He went on to win the 1994 Monaco Grand Prix.

The Monaco Grand Prix of 1989: the familiar yellow helmet of the legendary Ayrton Senna, who is driving a McLaren MP4/5 Honda in first position at Portier. It's not uncommon for the cars to clip the barriers with their rear wheels when negotiating this particular corner.

the person or persons in front, those beside them, and of course praying hard that nobody hits them from the rear!

To come out of this bend on the first lap in one piece is a small miracle in itself. If you are lucky enough to escape damage or collisions, then you will be accelerating hard uphill and left into Casino Square. A burst of exotic colours and beautiful buildings flashes past the drivers as they negotiate the square and dive downhill past the Hotel Metropole and on to the most complex part of the course.

Braking hard from some 200 kph, the next obstacle is Virage Mirabeau, a sharp right-hand bend

Graham Hill joined Team Lotus as a mechanic in the mid-1950s, and debuted in Formula One at the 1958 Monaco Grand Prix. He is shown here during the 1968 Monaco Grand Prix in his Lotus 49B Ford, in first position at Tabac. Hill went on to win his second world championship during this year.

A scene from the 2001 Monaco Grand Prix, showing cars on the entry to Rascasse (left) and also exiting Anthony Nogues (right), with the pit lane in between. The everyday one-way street signs can be easily spotted painted on the road.

that swoops down to Lowes, a left-hand hairpin – the steering needs to be turned at full lock here or you may well not make the turn, which would be very embarrassing. A further right turn takes you down further towards the waterfront and the Virage Portier, a sharp right-hand turning that takes you to the start of the tunnel. This is the fastest part of the circuit and cars reach some 270 kph plus. The noise is deafening and the cars exit the other end of the tunnel like bullets being propelled from a gun.

One more chicane and on towards the famous Virage du Bureau de Tabac, situated on the harbour front with all its exotic million-dollar yachts. Their owners watch the race with champagne glass in one hand and a pretty girl at their side. The swimming pool area – la Piscine – is negotiated via several nasty kinks, a section of the circuit that was revised in 1997 with a view to making it safer.

The Virage de la Rascasse follows quickly, taken at a snail's pace of just 30 kph – it is the slowest part of the circuit. The drivers then negotiate a short straight and into a fast right-hand bend – Virage Anthony Noghes (dedicated to the founder of the race) – before stamping on the accelerator to complete their first lap . . . only another seventy-seven to go!

Olivier Panis rounds Rascasse during the 2002 Monaco Grand Prix. Rascasse has had several modifications over the years. In 1973 the track from Tabac to La Rascasse was re-profiled to make way for the new swimming pool and later Ste. Devote and Rascasse corners were tightened in an attempt to slow the cars down.

BRITISH GRAND PRIX

Venue: Silverstone, Northamptonshire, Great Britain

The British Grand Prix has not always been held at the renowned Silverstone circuit, its current home. Several other venues have also had the privilege of holding this event, and in particular Aintree and Brands Hatch.

Today the three-day racing event is part of the FIA Formula One World Championship, and attracts a great deal of attention, with spectators arriving from all parts of the world. Recently the venue has had to upgrade its facilities in order to remain the host circuit, and it narrowly escaped losing its place on the calendar in 2009 before signing a new contract to hold the prestigious race for many years to come.

Grand Prix racing was brought to people's attention way back in 1926 by Henry Segrave, a British national who was born in Baltimore, Maryland, USA of an American mother and an Irish father. He attended Eton College in England and served in the British Royal Air Force in the First World War as a fighter pilot.

In 1923 he won the French Grand Prix and the following year the San Sebastian Grand Prix at the Lasarte Circuit, Spain, driving a Sunbeam. Following one other win at Miramas in France, he retired from racing to concentrate on speed records, having become the first British driver to win a Grand Prix in a British car.

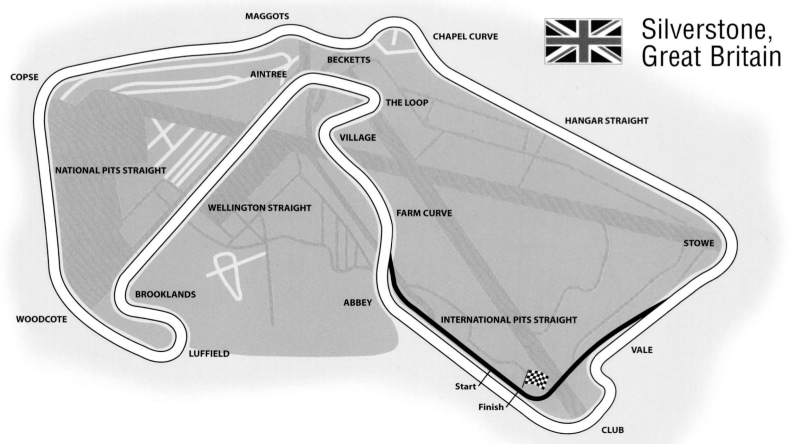

Silverstone, Great Britain

The first British Grand Prix took place at the Brooklands Circuit near Weybridge in Surrey, England. The circuit was opened on 17 June 1907 and was the first custom-built banked race circuit in the world. The banking was nearly thirty feet high in places and along the centre of the track ran a dotted

Kimi Räikkönen in a McLaren Mercedes leads the chasing pack during the 2006 British Grand Prix. The landmark British Racing Drivers' Clubhouse in the heart of the Silverstone Formula One circuit, completed for the Grand Prix of 2000, can be seen in the background.

black line, known as the 'Fifty Foot Line'. By driving over the line a driver could theoretically take the banked corners without having to use the steering wheel. The first British Grand Prix of 1926 was won by the French team, which consisted of Louis Wagner and Robert Sénéchal, driving a Delage 155B.

Brooklands also held the event the following year when Robert Benoist won in a Delage, after which it moved to the old Donington race circuit near Castle Donington, Leicestershire, England. It was held here from 1935 through to 1938 when the race was won two years running by both Alfa Romeo (1935, 1936) and Auto Union (1937, 1938). With the onset of the Second World War, racing was interrupted and

The first British Grand Prix took place at the Banked Brooklands circuit in 1926. Seen here is a very excited Robert Benoist – who won the race the following year – in his Delage 15S8. His reserve driver, Robert Sénéchal, is seen holding the flowers on the left of the car.

The first-ever British Grand Prix, run in 1926 at the Brooklands circuit, was won by the French team of Louis Wagner and Robert Sénéchal, both driving a Delage 155B. Seen here is the start of that race with Albert Divo in a Talbot 700 in the lead. Note the 'Fifty Foot' line around the top of the track.

Grand Prix racing didn't get going again until 1948, when it was staged for the first time at Silverstone.

Many race circuits in England have their roots as RAF air bases, the runway and related connecting roads being used for the race track itself. Silverstone is no exception and as Donington Park was in disrepair and Brooklands was taken over by the aircraft industry, it was decided by the Royal Automobile Club to use the Silverstone outer taxiways and interconnecting runways as the home for the British Grand Prix in 1948. There was little

money around to carry out extensive work after the war, so a makeshift pit area was designated and straw bales were placed strategically on corners. The circuit was 3.7 miles long and became popular with people wanting to have some fun and get away from the post-war depression. The 1948 event was won by the Maserati of Gigi Villoresi, who beat fellow Italian Alberto Ascari. The following year the circuit was changed and became the basis of what it is today, with the Maserati of Emanuel de Graffenried taking the honours.

The original Donington race track was opened in 1931 and the British Grand Prix was held there in 1937 and 1938. Seen here in 1937 is a Mercedes-Benz W125 leading the eventual winner Bernd Rosemeyer in an Auto Union C type. Hermann Muller, also in an Auto Union, is chasing hard. The original Melbourne loop can be seen in the background.

The Silverstone circuit was originally an airfield and this picture demonstrates that quite clearly. The old oil drums seen at the side of the circuit were used to mark out the track. Luigi 'Gigi' Villoresi is leading Alberto Ascari, both driving a Maserati 4CLT48. They finished in first and second positions respectively.

The year 1950 saw the inauguration of the official Formula One World Championship, and Silverstone was chosen to host the very first round. The giants of motor racing turned up to do battle for the very first Formula One prize. A crowd of over 100,000 came to watch the spectacle in the presence of King George VI and his family. At the start of the race, the front of the grid was dominated by the Alfettas of Farina, Fangio and Fagioli, with pre-war drivers such as Chiron and Etancelin not too far behind. When the flag was waved for the start, Fangio immediately took the lead, and held it until his engine blew up eight laps from the end. This made way for second man 'Nino' Farina to take the prize in his Alfa, only to be followed by Luigi Fagioli and local driver Reg Parnell, both also driving Alfas, and so recording an Alfa Romeo 1-2-3. The event

July 11 1964 saw the British Grand Prix take place for the first time at the Brands Hatch circuit in Kent. Jim Clark in a Lotus 25 Climax had posted fastest lap and grabbed pole position. At the start of the race Graham Hill (BRM P261) and Dan Gurney (Brabham BT7-Climax) lead, while Frank Gardner (Brabham BT10-Ford) is seen crashing at the rear of the pack.

The concentration can clearly be seen on the face of Mike Hawthorn as he guides his Ferrari 625 round the Aintree circuit, Liverpool. The 1955 British Grand Prix was eventually won by the young English driver Stirling Moss in a Mercedes-Benz. It was the first time an Englishman had won the race. Mike Hawthorn came in sixth.

had been a huge success and confirmed the popularity of the race series.

In 1951 the British Racing Drivers' Club (BRDC) took on the lease from the RAC and promptly instigated changes to the circuit. The pit area was moved from Farm straight to the straight between Woodcote and Copse, and a further short circuit was designed within the Grand Prix circuit.

The race remained at Silverstone up to 1955, when it was held at the Aintree circuit, alternating between the two after that. Brands Hatch was first used in 1964 and alternated with Silverstone from then onwards; Aintree was never used again as a Grand Prix venue.

Brands Hatch is situated in the countryside near West Kingsdown in Kent, England. It too has a

In 1952 the Grand Prix was still being staged at Silverstone, and Alberto Ascari in his Ferrari 500 crossed the finishing line first. Here he is seen leading the group headed by Giuseppe Farina in another Ferrari 500 at the start of the race.

The Lotus of Jim Clark seen on pole position during the 1964 British Grand Prix at Brands Hatch. Clark sits patiently in his Lotus 25 Climax prior to the start of the race, which he went on to win.

grand history of Formula One racing and boasts some of the most exciting races in the sport. Unfortunately it has also seen some terrible and fatal crashes. The original race track was used for bicycle and then motorcycle grass track racing, and when Brands Hatch Stadium Ltd was formed in 1947, a one-mile oval course suitable for cars was created. The track continued to expand in 1954, with the addition of Druid's Bend, lengthening the circuit to 1.24 miles, while pits and spectator banks were added too. The purchase of a grandstand from the Northolt trotting track in 1955 was another addition.

The 2.65 mile Grand Prix circuit was constructed in 1959, and the non-championship Silver City Trophy Formula One race was the first major event to take place at the circuit in 1960. Just four years later it hosted the 1964 Formula One World Championship British Grand Prix – also given the title of RAC European Grand Prix. The race was won by Jim Clark in a Lotus Climax, with Graham Hill in a BRM hard on his heels in second place, and John Surtees in a Ferrari taking third spot. From here onwards the race was held on alternate years with Silverstone. The fearful Paddock Hill Bend claimed the lives of George Crossman, Tony Flory and Stuart Duncan, and other serious accidents happened in a very short period during the mid-sixties. In 1971 Jo Siffert was tragically killed in an end-of-season, non-championship, Formula One race at Brands Hatch. The suspension of his BRM had been damaged during a first lap incident with Ronnie Peterson, and had then broken during the

Brands Hatch, Great Britain

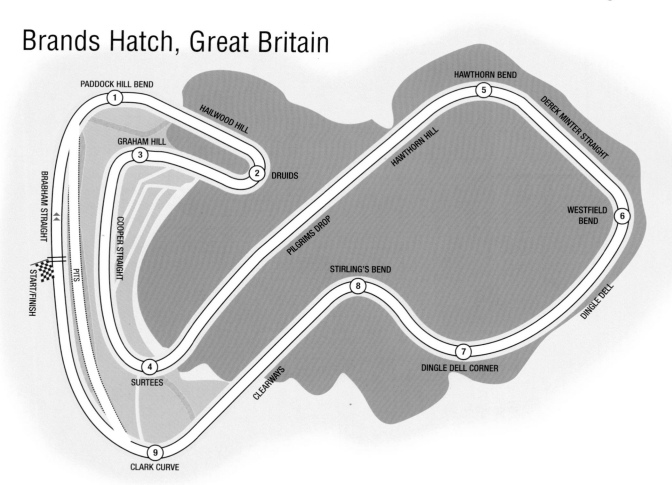

By the 1980s, the Brands Hatch circuit had been updated and upgraded in line with other circuits. There was now a dedicated pit area and facilities that would happily accommodate the faster cars and all their entourage. Here, Nelson Piquet leads from the start in the 1986 race.

The Williams team dominated the British Grand Prix in the 1990s, winning six times – 1991, 1992, 1993, 1994, 1996 and 1997 – on a revised Silverstone circuit. Seen here at the 1991 race is winner Nigel Mansell giving Ayrton Senna a lift back to the pits after he had run out of fuel.

As can be clearly seen here, Hanger Straight at Silverstone is a great place to overtake. James Hunt (McLaren M26 Ford) leads John Watson (Brabham BT45B Alfa Romeo), Jody Scheckter (Wolf WR1 Ford), Niki Lauda (Ferrari 312T2), Gunnar Nilsson and Mario Andretti (both Lotus 78 Fords) at the 1977 British Grand Prix.

race. As so often happened in those days, Siffert's BRM crashed heavily, caught fire and he couldn't get out of the burning car. The last British Grand Prix to be held at Brands Hatch was in 1986, with victory going to Nigel Mansell.

From then onwards and up to the present day, Silverstone has been the home of the official British Grand Prix. Much work has been done to the facilities and surrounding area, giving better access and more modern amenities.

The BRDC purchased the entire 720 acre Silverstone plot in 1971, and commenced a redevelopment programme which saw the track being upgraded. The 1975 British Grand Prix meeting saw a chicane introduced, in a bid to control the speeds through the very fast Woodcote Corner.

Some welcome additions to race circuits today are the large, strategically placed screens. During the 2006 Grand Prix at Silverstone, for example, these allowed the spectators to watch Kimi Räikkönen making a pit stop whilst Michael Schumacher in his Ferrari was leading the race.

Over the past few years the Silverstone circuit has gone through major upgrading, with new hospitality suites and stands, a redesigned track layout and new pit and paddock facilities. Here, as Fernando Alonso screams away from the start line, the old pit facilities can be seen in the background.

In 1987 a deviation was made at Bridge Corner, and during 1990 and 1991 the whole track underwent a major redesign. The first race on the new track configuration proved to be a memorable one in which Nigel Mansell crossed the finishing line of his home Grand Prix in first place. The crowd went wild with excitement, and on his victory lap Mansell even found time to stop and give his arch rival, Ayrton Senna, a lift back to the pits, his car having expired during the later part of the race. With excessively high speeds being attained during the late 1980s, a corner was introduced prior to Woodcote, with the other corners also being attended to.

It was announced by F1 supremo Bernie Ecclestone in 2008 that the British Grand Prix would no longer be staged at the Northamptonshire circuit. A decision was made that 2009 would be the last year of the Grand Prix at the Silverstone circuit, and the following year it would move to the East Midlands Donington race circuit. However, the funds for the required redevelopment at Donington were not raised, and the race is currently contracted to a revamped Silverstone until at least 2027.

Silverstone underwent some dramatic changes before the 2010 Formula One race, including a new 'Arena' layout where the drivers turn infield at Abbey before rejoining the old circuit at Brooklands. The relocated and modernized pit and paddock complex known as 'The Wing' was opened in 2011.

An aerial view of the Silverstone circuit during the 2006 Grand Prix, showing the well-covered grandstands and circuit layout.

The crowds at Silverstone for the British Grand Prix – all manner of flags denote the various supporters from many countries around the world.

CANADIAN GRAND PRIX

Venue: Circuit Gilles Villeneuve, Montreal, Canada

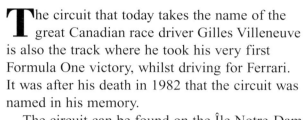

The circuit that today takes the name of the great Canadian race driver Gilles Villeneuve is also the track where he took his very first Formula One victory, whilst driving for Ferrari. It was after his death in 1982 that the circuit was named in his memory.

The circuit can be found on the Île Notre-Dame, a man-made island in the St Lawrence River, just minutes from Montreal. Although during the rest of the year the island is a tranquil and pleasant place to be, the Grand Prix weekend brings noise, unusually large crowds and a frenzy of activity. This is supposedly the most watched Formula One race in the world and in 2005 was the third most watched event on the planet.

Although classed as a street circuit, it is very different from Monaco, for example. It is a very fast track and yet still has areas that have barriers close to the circuit. On the exit to the final chicane is a wall, on which is written 'Bienvenue au Québec' (Welcome to Quebec), which has taken the nickname of the Quebec Wall. Several World Champion drivers have ended their race after confronting the wall, which has been renamed the 'Wall of Champions'.

Few people would disagree that the Canadian Grand Prix is one of the most popular motoring events, and spectators come from around the world to take part in the weekend of celebrations. But to the horror of regular race-goers worldwide, it was announced in 2008 that the Grand Prix would not be included on the 2009 schedule, due to 'contractual problems'. These were overcome in time for the 2010 season, and racing resumed until at least 2014.

Circuit Gilles Villeneuve, Canada

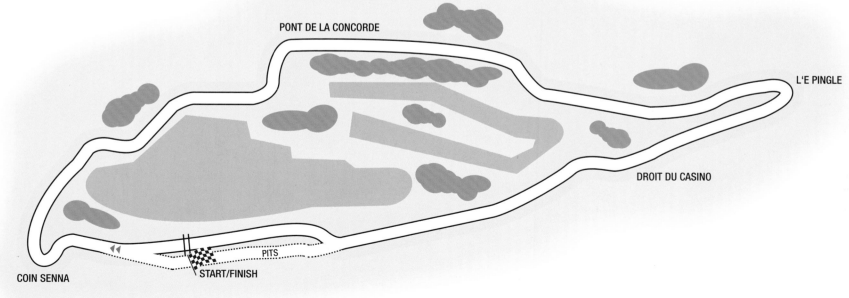

The Canadian Grand Prix is run on the Île Notre-Dame, which is situated on the Saint Lawrence River. The building in the background is the Montreal Casino, which was originally built as the French and Quebec Pavilions for Expo 67. Starting another lap is eventual 2006 Canadian Grand Prix winner Fernando Alonso, driving a Renault R26.

Montreal and its skyscrapers can be clearly seen in the background as Jenson Button (Honda RA106) attempts to capture pole position in the practice session for the 2006 Formula One Grand Prix.

Here the Montreal Biosphère, formerly the American Pavilion of Expo 67, can be seen on the adjacent Île Sainte-Hélène. Heading towards L'Epingle during practice for the 2006 Canadian Grand Prix is Rubens Barrichello in a Honda RA106.

Although Jacques Villeneuve, son of the late Gilles, is a main attraction, his father still has a following that any driver would give their right arm for. He is the local hero and along with the tifosi from Ferrari, makes this a motor racing weekend not to be missed.

The circuit has been changed over the years. For example, the pits have been moved from one end of the island to the other. Some of the twisty corners have, also been ironed out, creating a high-speed circuit. Undoubtedly now a fast track, a few of the drivers agree that it lacks some of the challenge of high-speed corners. In 1994, in order to slow the cars down, a temporary chicane was installed before the Casino turn, which was subsequently removed in 1996 to make way for the current Casino straight.

The year 2002 saw some important changes made to the circuit at the request of the FIA: the east hairpin was shortened by thirty metres, a new pit exit was designed, and the Senna curves were enlarged by two metres. The race was also extended from sixty-nine to seventy laps, a total distance of 305.27 km.

Some strange things have happened here too. In 1991, on the last lap, and before the chequered flag was waved, Nigel Mansell (Williams), whilst saluting the crowd stalled his engine and had to retire from the race, leaving Nelson Piquet (Benetton) to claim his third victory in Montreal.

At the end of an incredible race, Frenchman Jean Alesi (Ferrari) recorded the only victory of his career in front of a delirious crowd in 1995, only to

In 1999 this corner became well known for catching out former World Champions Damon Hill, Michael Schumacher and Jacques Villeneuve, who all crashed into it. The slogan Bienvenue au Québec translates as 'Welcome to Quebec'. Here, Nico Rosberg in his Williams FW28 Cosworth is safely past the corner.

break down during the victory lap and return to the pits riding on Michael Schumacher's car.

The circuit has also seen its bad days. In 1982 it witnessed a terrible accident when Riccardo Paletti slammed into the rear of Didier Pironi's stalled car on the starting grid. Although rushed to hospital, Paletti later died of his injuries. Olivier Panis also had a huge accident in 1997, when he spun off the circuit and broke both his legs, bringing the race to a premature end.

Just over forty years ago the piece of land that is Mosport Park raceway was a farm. It was hard to imagine that one day it would host some of the most important motor races in the world. Although Mosport Park had held races prior to the Formula One event coming there, it had suffered severe financial problems. The track was bought out of receivership by Cantrack Motor Racing Ltd in 1966, and just one year later in 1967 Canada joined the Formula One circus, as Mosport hosted the first

Canadian Grand Prix. Although a miserably rainy day, some 58,000 people came to watch the racing and saw Jack Brabham take the very first Formula One Grand Prix victory in Canada. All types of motor racing have been held at the circuit – Can Am series, IndyCar, USAC stock car races and even motorcycle racing. From this point onwards, the Grand Prix alternated for the next few years with the Mont-Tremblant circuit in Quebec, although that circuit was abandoned due to safety problems in the early 1970s. Mosport then became the permanent home of the Canadian Grand Prix until 1978, when it was moved to the present location of the Île Notre-Dame, Montreal. Mosport Park is located in the woodlands near Lake Ontario and has fast sweeping bends that follow the contours of the land. Many thought it was just too dangerous for Formula One racing cars, but with its wonderfully demanding corners it soon attained a reputation for being a driver's circuit. The last Formula One race victory

Mosport Park Road Course, Canada

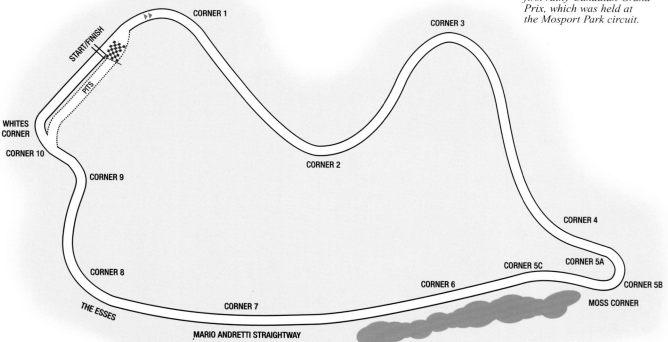

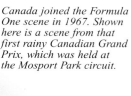

Canada joined the Formula One scene in 1967. Shown here is a scene from that first rainy Canadian Grand Prix, which was held at the Mosport Park circuit.

came in 1977, with Jody Scheckter taking the prize for the Wolf racing team. Although Mosport is no longer used by the Formula One teams, it still holds important races throughout the year.

If you are a racing fanatic you might like to consider visiting several other circuits near the Île Notre-Dame, Montreal circuit. For example Watkins Glen is only about two hours away in New York State, USA. Both Canada's Trois Rivières circuit and the picturesque Mont-Tremblant track are not that far away either and well worth a visit.

Seen here at the Mosport Park circuit during the 1969 Canadian Grand Prix is Pedro Rodriguez in a Ferrari 312. He retired with oil pressure problems. The circuit was surrounded by fields and wooded areas and there were few barriers.

Set amidst the scenic Laurentian mountains, Mont-Tremblant circuit is quite stunning. In the two Canadian Grand Prix events staged here, and out of forty cars entered, only sixteen finished due to a high attrition rate. Here in the 1968 Grand Prix John Surtees (Honda RA301) leads Jackie Stewart (Matra MS10 Ford) and Jack Brabham (Brabham BT26 Repco).

US GRAND PRIX

Venue: Indianapolis Motor Speedway, Indianapolis, Indiana, USA

The Indianapolis Motor Speedway in Indianapolis, USA, often referred to as 'The Brickyard', because the surface was originally made up of over three million bricks, is not just a racing venue. To American racing fans, it is a place of pilgrimage, a shrine. There are many Americans who wouldn't have bothered to raise an eyebrow for the Formula One event that took place from 2000 until 2007; to them it's just not the kind of racing they enjoy – give them the Indy 500, 365 days of the year and they would be happy to die there!

With an overall capacity for 400,000 spectators, it's the largest sporting venue in the world and was placed on the National Register of Historic Places in

1975 and designated a National Historic Landmark in 1987. It is the second-oldest surviving automobile race track in the world (after the Milwaukee Mile), having existed since 1909.

The first Indy 500 race took place in 1911, and when the Formula One Championship started in 1950, the Indy 500 became one of the rounds. However, except for Alberto Ascari in 1952, no regular Formula One drivers attended these races. It wasn't until seven years later that an official Formula One event would be held in the US, and the top drivers of the day would participate too.

The American Grand Prix series of races, attended by top European drivers alongside

 ## Indianapolis Motor Speedway, USA

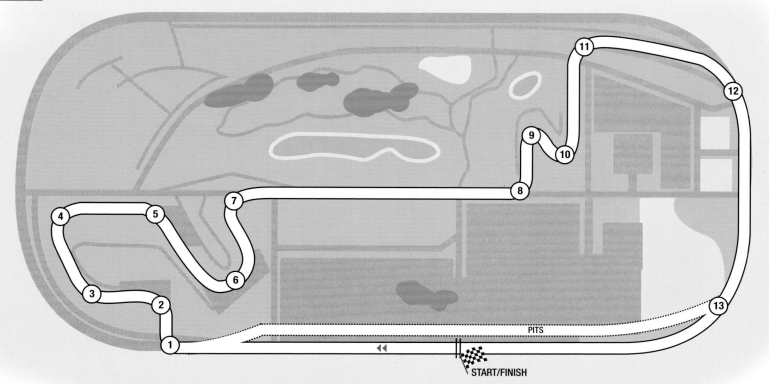

Indianapolis Motor Speedway is the second-oldest surviving automobile racing track in the world, after the Milwaukee Mile. This is a familiar sight for many Americans, and the circuit was the venue for the US Formula One Grand Prix from 2000 until 2007. Seen here is Nico Rosberg leading Vitantino Liuzzi and heading for the start/finish line during the 2006 race.

It was Russian-born Alec Ulmann who organized the first Formula One American Grand Prix on the road course at Sebring in Florida in December 1959. Although the picture shows how exciting the race was, attendance was poor. Jack Brabham fights his Cooper T-51 Climax as it desperately tries to get out of shape. Bruce McLaren can be seen chasing hard.

American drivers, held a United States Grand Prix in 1908 and again from 1910 through to 1916. The First World War brought motor racing to a temporary close and it would never be the same after the conflict.

The Russian-born Alec Ulmann organized the first official Formula One Grand Prix, which took place on the road course at Sebring in Florida in December 1959. The starting grid included seven American drivers, but it was New Zealand's Bruce McLaren in a Cooper who took his first win in Formula One, and at the same time became the youngest driver ever to win a Grand Prix. But despite being a thrilling event the race didn't attract the crowds and Ulmann moved the venue the following year. The race was held at the Riverside

One could say – third time lucky! When the race was moved to the Watkins Glen circuit in New York state it became a great success and was well attended every year. In the 1965 event, Lorenzo Bandini driving a Ferrari 1512 leads Jochen Rindt in a Cooper T77 Climax. They finished in 4th and 6th positions respectively.

By moving the race to the Riverside International Raceway in California in 1960, Ulmann was sure that there would be better crowd attendance. Unfortunately, he was wrong. The start of the 1960 race shows Jack Brabham (Cooper T53 Climax) leading Dan Gurney (BRM P48), Stirling Moss (Lotus 18 Climax), Jo Bonnier (BRM P48) and Innes Ireland (Lotus 18 Climax).

International Raceway in Riverside, California. This time it was Stirling Moss who took the honours after securing pole position. Receipts were still not good and so the event once again became a one-off.

For 1961, Cameron Argetsinger, sports car enthusiast, lawyer and auto racing executive, was asked to host the Grand Prix at Watkins Glen in New York State. The circuit already hosted motor races and was well established as a racing venue. This time the crowds came and in fact Watkins Glen became a favourite of both fans and drivers, with some spectacular racing taking place in the wooded hills of upstate New York.

The Glen, as it was fondly known, also had its characters, of which one was the official starter. 'Tex' Hopkins, generally seen wearing a lavender suit and with cigar in mouth, would stand in front of the waiting pack, and with an exaggerated jump would wave the green flag to start the race. The winner of the race would also be greeted by Tex once again jumping in the air and thrashing his

Long Beach, California, 1977: Jody Scheckter, driving a Wolf WR1 Ford, leads Mario Andretti in a Lotus 78 Ford and future World Champion Niki Lauda in a Ferrari 312T2 out of Le Gasomet into Shoreline Drive.

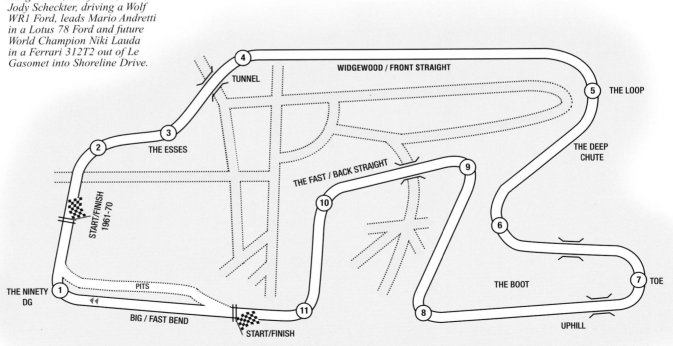

Watkins Glen International, USA

Long Beach, California, USA

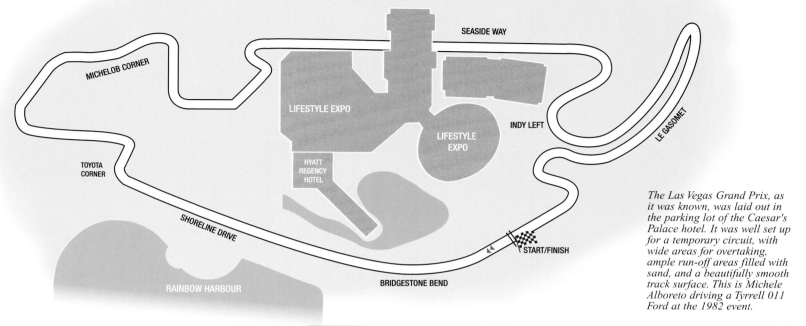

The Las Vegas Grand Prix, as it was known, was laid out in the parking lot of the Caesar's Palace hotel. It was well set up for a temporary circuit, with wide areas for overtaking, ample run-off areas filled with sand, and a beautifully smooth track surface. This is Michele Alboreto driving a Tyrrell 011 Ford at the 1982 event.

chequered flag around. Prior to the 1971 race, several significant changes were made to the circuit, which increased its length from 2.35 miles to 3.38 miles. Four new corners were added in a new section known as the 'Boot' or 'Anvil', the new layout leaving the old circuit near the southern end in a curling, downhill, left-hand turn through the woods. Skirting the edge of the hillside it hit two right-hand corners, which were positioned over a blind crest, leading into a left-hander and then returning back to the old track. Besides this, the track was resurfaced and widened, whilst the pit area and start/finish line were moved back prior to the sharp right-hander known as 'the 90'. But no matter how much work would be done, by the mid-1970s the Glen was not only declining in popularity, but a few horrendous, sometimes fatal accidents began to tarnish its image. The increasingly faster and stiffer ground-effect cars of the era finally led to the Glen's exit from the Formula One calendar, with Alan Jones winning the last race in 1980 for Williams.

One could be forgiven for the confusion now but the US, like Italy, suddenly had two Grand Prix

The Formula One United States Grand Prix was held on the Phoenix downtown street circuit in Arizona between 1989-91. It was only run for three years due to lack of spectator interest. This is a great aerial view of the road circuit taken during the last race in 1991.

races being run over the year. Between 1976 and 1980 the Glen races were known as the United States Grand Prix East, whilst a new race, taking place at Long Beach, California, was known as the United States Grand Prix West. The US GP West races were part of the championship between 1976 and 1983, and were a great success from day one. Americans loved to compare it with Monaco, as it was laid out on the streets of downtown Long Beach. The circuit layout changed several times during its eight-year reign, but always incorporated the long sweeping right-hander down the infamous Shoreline Drive along the waterfront. But once again the circuit was unable to cope with the increasingly high speeds of the cars, along with a few financial problems. In 1983, John Watson won the final race after starting in 22nd position on the grid.

With the Glen giving up the Formula One title in 1980, a new venue was chosen, this time in Las Vegas. The Formula One championship was only run here in 1981 and 1982, with the desert heat putting off both drivers and spectators. It was to run in the car park of Caesar's Palace hotel, was well designed for a temporary circuit and wide enough for overtaking, and even had sandy run-off areas. The track surface itself was also in excellent condition, but one problem for the drivers was that it ran anti-clockwise and put tremendous pressure on their necks. It didn't draw great crowds and so when Michele Alboreto won the 1982 race in his Tyrrell, the curtain also came down on the Vegas race.

For 1984, the United States Grand Prix moved to Dallas, Texas, with the track being laid out on the streets surrounding the Texas State Fair. However, with damage being sustained during a support race and with the oppressive heat causing the track further wear, the race was largely considered a disaster and Formula One did not return there.

The official Formula One championship returned to the United States in 1989, when it was moved to Phoenix, Arizona. Once again it was a street circuit laid out in downtown Phoenix. It was unpopular both with drivers and the local crowd, and after the 1991 race, at which only about 18,000 spectators turned up, Formula One shipped out and did not return to the United States until 2000.

It was now time for the Formula One circus to move to 'The Brickyard' – Indianapolis Motor Speedway. Not everybody was convinced, and with Formula One racing going through a bit of a downturn and Americans still wondering what all this Formula One business was about, it all looked a little bit of a gamble. Still, the teams turned up and without doubt the venue and its amazing facilities were more than adequate to take on the race and all that went with it.

The 2.606 mile infield track, which included one mile of the oval circuit, was prepared and the cars ran in a clockwise direction. The first meeting in 2000 saw a crowd of approximately 225,000 – a record at the time for Formula One attendance – and Michael Schumacher won the race in his Ferrari.

The following year the event took place just three weeks after the 9/11 disaster, and security was at its highest. Many teams wore tributes to the United States on their helmets and cars. The 2005 race was a farce as only six cars, shod with Bridgestone tyres, actually raced. This was due to a problem encountered with the Michelin tyres and so the teams using Michelin tyres were unable to take part in the race. Many people, in particular those who had spent large amounts of money attending the

Keke Rosberg (Williams FW09 Honda) survived a brutal battle of attrition and scored his only win of the season at the dramatic, unpredictable, one-time-only Dallas Grand Prix of 1984. The tight and twisty course was laid out on the Texas State Fair Grounds and featured two hairpin curves. Extremely high temperatures were instrumental in breaking up the track after only a few laps.

The 2006 Indy race was something of a dull affair, with little overtaking and a predictable race result. The first lap accidents, which took out seven cars, didn't help the situation. At Turn 1 Mark Webber collided with Christian Klien, who then spun around and was taken out by Franck Montagny. At Turn 2 Juan Pablo Montoya nudged his team-mate Kimi Räikkönen into a spin. Montoya then clouted Jenson Button, whose front right tyre got caught by BMW-Sauber's Nick Heidfeld, who in turn was launched into a spectacular triple barrel roll. Montoya also caught Scuderia Toro Rosso's Scott Speed in the incident. None of the drivers were injured.

race, were angered by the situation and there were lots of questions being asked of the race, and whether it would ever be run again. But it was run again in 2006, with the Ferrari of Michael Schumacher taking the chequered flag and claiming yet another victory.

The Indy Circuit is probably the best-known race track in the world, with the Indy 500 race being transmitted all over the world. Only a small part of the actual oval circuit is used, with the main part being on the infield, but on the long straight, which incorporates the banking, the cars will go full throttle and reach speeds of 350 kph. One circuit length is 4.192 km, total laps run in the race are 73, and a distance of 306.016 km is covered. Visitors also get a great view of the track, from pretty well

any part of the circuit they are allowed to visit, with huge grandstands overlooking the main straight. The oval itself has also undergone some changes in the last few years – all in the interests of increased safety. The US Grand Prix has always been precarious, and in 2007 Bernie Ecclestone signalled the end. He said an agreement with Indianapolis could not be concluded, to the regret of both parties. There was mention that possibly in the future the race could return, but this looks very unlikely after the purpose-built Circuit of the Americas near Austin, Texas, began hosting the official US Grand Prix in 2012. Also, there will once again be two races in the USA, with plans for another event, called the Grand Prix of America, to take place through the streets of New Jersey beginning in 2014.

Fernando Alonso, driving a Renault R26, leads his team-mate Giancarlo Fisichella around the infamous Turn 13 – the high-speed last corner before the start/finish straight at the 2006 USA Grand Prix.

ABU DHABI GRAND PRIX

Venue: Yas Marina Circuit, Abu Dhabi, UAE

During 2009, some significant changes were to make a deep impression on the world of Formula One racing. Not only was the sport preparing for an overhaul, but an unprecedented worldwide recession was also helping to change the sport and its entourage for the foreseeable future. The Honda racing team for example, made the decision not to contest the 2009 season, although the team was later bought-out by Ross Brawn. He became the new principle and also secured an engine supply deal with Mercedes-Benz. At the same time one country, oil-rich Abu Dhabi, was about to join the circus with a new venue.

With the recent introduction of the race in Singapore that took place at night, the Abu Dhabi circuit is even more spectacular as the race starts during daylight hours and finishes when the sun has set.

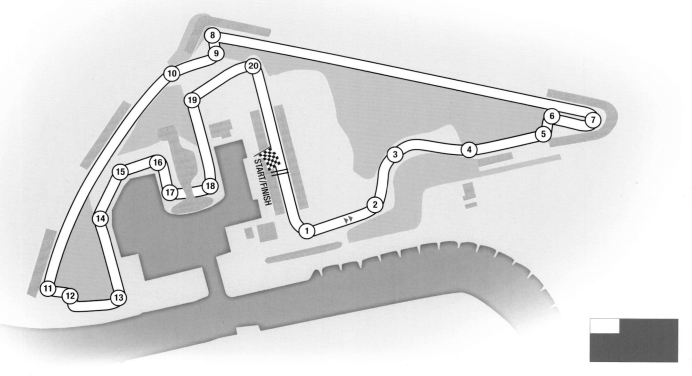

Yas Marina Circuit, Abu Dhabi, UAE

The new 5.55 km (3.5 miles) circuit was, as ever, designed by the Herrman Tilke company and encompasses a mix of sandy dunes and an exotic marina.

The track, located on the beautiful Yas Island, on the eastern side of Abu Dhabi, features nine right turns and eleven left turns, with top speeds reaching 320 kph (200 mph) and an average of 198 kph (124 mph). Unlike most of the other circuits, it runs in an anti-clockwise direction.

As far as spectators and teams are concerned, all the grandstands are covered, protecting people from the excessively hot desert sun, whilst the pit area is designed with 40 garages. With the strategically positioned 500-room Yas Marina Hotel and the solar-powered Sun tower straddling the track,

The Yas Marina Circuit, situated on Yas Island and opened in 2009, has many viewing areas, all beautifully covered and protected from the heat of the day.

Resembling a Monaco in the desert, the Abu Dhabi circuit is a paradise for race goers. In 2012 the race was won by the Finnish driver Kimi Räikkönen.

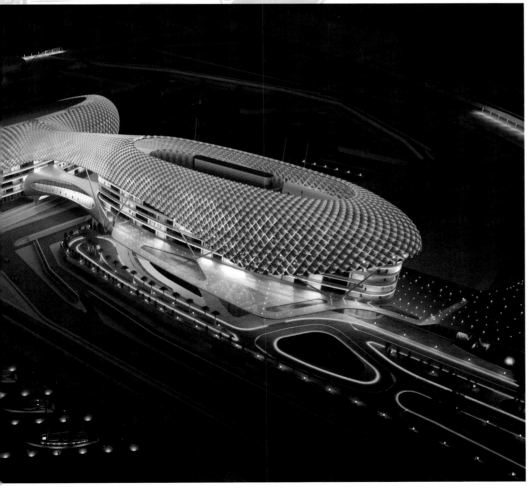

there is also no lack of accomodation or viewing areas around the circuit.

All in all, this is a wonderful circuit that incorporates a variety of racing styles with its high-speed sections, tight corners and even a twisty street-style segment. It is yet another of the new breed of fast, safe and beautifully accommodating race venues of the 21st century.

FRENCH GRAND PRIX

Venue: Circuit de Nevers Magny-Cours, Magny-Cours, France

The first World Championships were organized in 1925, and featured the French Grand Prix, Italian Grand Prix, Belgian Grand Prix and the Indianapolis 500. The French Grand Prix has been part of the Formula One championships since its inception in 1950, with the race being held at various race tracks throughout France. Only once, in 1955, did the race not take place, and since 1991 it has had its permanent home at the Circuit de Nevers Magny-Cours. The move to Magny-Cours was seen by the French government as an attempt to stimulate the economy of the area, but there is no doubt that it is a somewhat remote area of the country and many within the Formula One world have voiced that view. Due to financial difficulties, and the addition of new and modern circuits joining the calendar, the 2004 and 2005 races were put in doubt. They did go ahead though, as did the 2006 race. Sadly the 2009 French Grand Prix was cancelled after the French Motorsport Federation (FFSA) withdrew its funding. It was also said that Bernie Ecclestone was not a great admirer of the circuit, which is seen by many as flat and rather monotonous, and was keen to see a race nearer the French Capital, Paris.

The French Grand Prix is the oldest Grand Prix race and was run from June 1906 near Le Mans. This was the first race to be called a Grand Prix and was won after two days and some 1,238 km by the Hungarian driver Ferenc Szisz, driving a Renault.

The Nevers Magny-Cours circuit is owned by the Conseil Général de la Nièvre, and is a vast complex

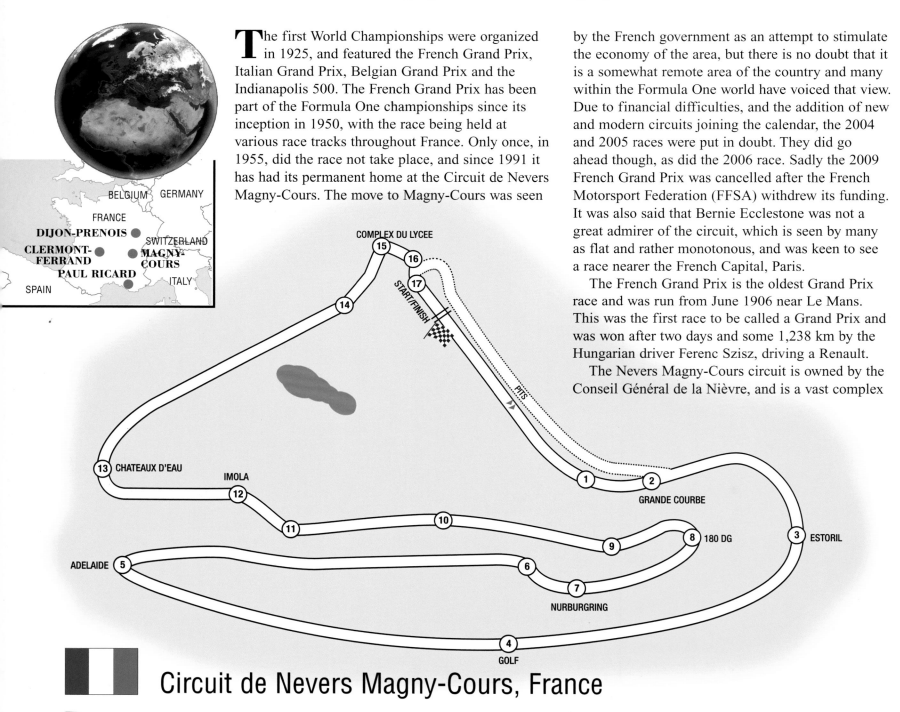

Circuit de Nevers Magny-Cours, France

An aerial view of the Magny-Cours circuit situated in the picturesque countryside of eastern France. It hosted the French Formula One Grand Prix from 1991 until 2008. The track, which is constantly up-dated, was re-designed in 2003 and is now used for a wide range of motoring events.

geared up for international motor racing events. The circuit was set up by the local Mayor, Jean Bernigaud, back in the 1950s. In 1959 a karting track was opened and two years later the official inauguration of the two-kilometre, Jean Behra track took place. Over the next twenty or so years the circuit became larger, and the area was further revitalized after a visit from President Mitterrand in 1988. The following year saw the inauguration of the new Magny-Cours circuit and the first French

A view of the start of the 2006 French Grand Prix at the Circuit Nevers de Magny-Cours: drivers slot into their positions as the front runner Felipe Massa (Ferrari 248F1) leads Fernando Alonso (Renault R26) and Jarno Trulli (Toyota TF106B) to the Estoril corner.

Formula One Grand Prix took place there in 1991. Since then it has become the official home of the Grand Prix, with buildings being upgraded, a new track for driving courses being added in 2000 and more updating being carried out to both circuit and buildings more recently. It is possible to visit the circuit on non-race days.The circuit also houses the Ligier Museum, which has a history of French Formula One racing. The Ligier team, including when it was taken over as the Prost team, was based there and used the track extensively in the 1990s for testing purposes. It is a very flat circuit with little in the way of uphill or downhill gradients, and there is little space for overtaking. Some would say that due

No mistaking which team these fans are supporting at the 2006 Grand Prix event! One or two Ferrari supporters mingle with the hordes of Renault fans. After all, Renault are World Champions and this is France!

As the start lights signal go, the drivers accelerate away from the start line and down towards the first bend at Grande Courbe. The 2006 French Grand Prix at the Circuit Nevers Magny-Cours leaps into action as Michael Schumacher in a Ferrari 248F1 and on pole position is closely tailed by his team-mate Felipe Massa.

to these factors the races here can be pretty uneventful. Many of the corners are named after other circuits and even though the final corner and chicane were modified in 2002, little change came out of it. It seems that the most exciting races that have taken place here have been in the wet, which is not unusual in the case of Formula One racing. The Grand Prix track technical details show that it is 4,411 metres long, 10.40 to 18 metres in width, the pits have forty-eight garages and the circuit has a maximum capacity of 148,000 of which 90,000 is for spectators. It is equipped for helicopter landings, medical and private, total track video coverage and emergency track warning lights systems. The circuit also comprises a karting track, an off-road track and the Piste Club. All in all, a pretty sophisticated and comprehensive layout.

Clermont-Ferrand ranks among the oldest cities of France and is situated in the Auvergne region.

The Charade Circuit is situated in the Auvergne mountains near Clermont-Ferrand and was built in 1958 around the flanks of an extinct volcano. Jochen Rindt (Lotus 49B-Ford) is seen approaching the start/finish area during the 1969 French Grand Prix.

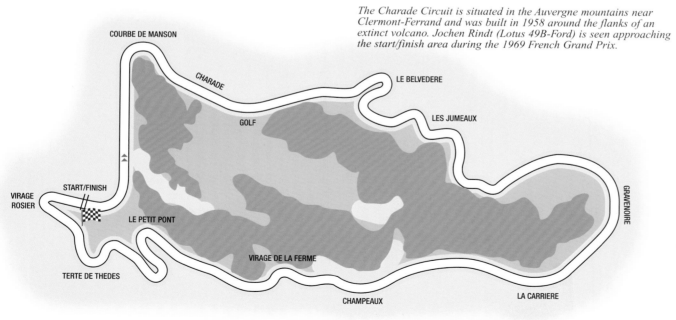

COURBE DE MANSON

CHARADE

LE BELVEDERE

GOLF

LES JUMEAUX

VIRAGE ROSIER

START/FINISH

GRAVENOIRE

LE PETIT PONT

VIRAGE DE LA FERME

LA CARRIERE

TERTE DE THEDES

CHAMPEAUX

Circuit de Charade, Clermont-Ferrand, France

Paul Ricard, Le Castellet, France

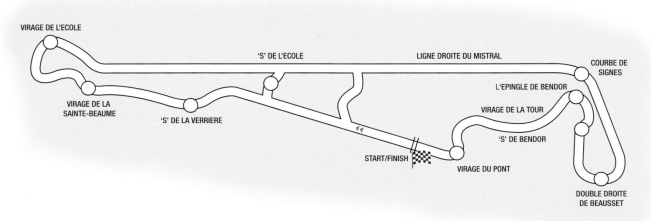

The Brabham BT7 Climax of Jo Bonnier leads Jo Siffert in a Brabham BT11 BRM around Le Petit Pont corner during the 1965 French Grand Prix at the Charade circuit.

A dramatic scene from the 1989 French Grand Prix at the Paul Ricard, Le Castellet circuit: Mauricio Gugelmin (March CG891 Judd) has a huge crash at Epingle Ecole at the start of the race, while Nigel Mansell (Ferrari) and team-mate Gerhard Berger gingerly pick their way past and Olivier Grouillard (Ligier-Cosworth) takes to the gravel in the background.

The French Grand Prix was run here in 1965, 1969, 1970 and 1972, with the circuit taking on several name descriptions. Many call it Clermont-Ferrand, but it also takes the name of Charade and the Circuit Louis Rosier. The circuit runs through the Auvergne mountains, and its twists and turns have even resulted in drivers complaining of motion sickness. Built in 1958 and stretching some 8.055 km (5.005 miles), it was seen as a faster version of the Nurburgring in Germany. The first Grand Prix to be held here was in 1965, and was won by Jim Clark in his Lotus-Climax. The following year saw the American film director John Frankenheimer make the film *Grand Prix* here, with 3,000 locals taking the part of spectators and mixing with celebrities such as Yves Montand and Françoise Hardy. The French Grand Prix was held here in 1969, 1970 and 1972, after which it moved to the new Paul Ricard circuit. Clermont Ferrand was built on the side of a hill and it proved difficult to keep the track clean, with stones causing all sorts of damage to cars and drivers. The idea of run-off areas was just not possible, due to the location. Although Formula Three, and though touring car, sports car and

De Dijon-Prenois, France

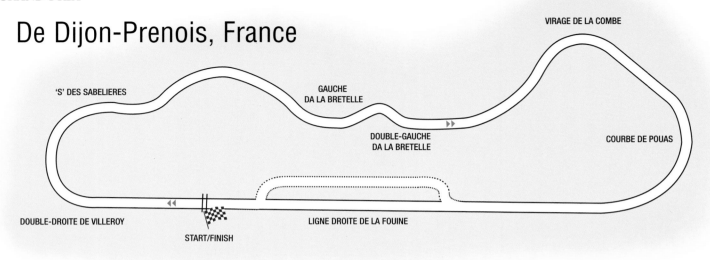

VIRAGE DE LA COMBE

'S' DES SABELIERES

GAUCHE
DA LA BRETELLE

DOUBLE-GAUCHE
DA LA BRETELLE

COURBE DE POUAS

DOUBLE-DROITE DE VILLEROY

START/FINISH

LIGNE DROITE DE LA FOUINE

rallying events did continue to be staged, the circuit was closed at the end of 1988.

Le Castellet-Paul Ricard (1971, 1973, 1975, 1976, 1978, 1980, 1982, 1983, 1985-1990) is tucked away in the hills above Marseilles. The circuit is generally referred to as Paul Ricard, although its real name is Le Castellet, after the village where it is located. It was built with finance from the drinks magnate Paul Ricard and opened in 1970, when it was considered by many to be the safest racing circuit in the world. It had great facilities and generally benefited from good weather, due to the location, and teams often took the opportunity to use the circuit for test sessions during the winter periods. Many French drivers gained their experience at this circuit and in 1971 it hosted its first Formula One Grand Prix, won by Jackie Stewart in his Tyrrell-Ford. The track is dominated by the mile-long Mistral straight – named after the local wind – which is followed rapidly by the very tight Signes corner. A few zig-zags before you take the Virage du Pont and slip into the start/finish

Built in 1972, Dijon-Prenois played host to the Formula One French Grand Prix five times and the Swiss Grand Prix once. Here John Watson (McLaren MP4/1 Ford) leads Nelson Piquet (Brabham BT49C Ford), Alain Prost (Renault RE30) and Jacques Laffite (Talbot Ligier JS17 Matra) at the start of the 1981 event.

straight. An 'S' bend, another corner and round the Virage de l'Ecole, before once again you find yourself flat out on the very fast Mistral straight. The full Grand Prix circuit was about 5.77 km (3.610 miles) in length, but was shortened in 1986 to 3.79 km (2.369 miles) and named the GP short circuit. The shortening of the circuit was due to the fatal accident of Elio de Angelis, who was killed whilst testing the Brabham BT55. The last French Formula One Grand Prix to be held at the Paul Ricard was in 1990, after which it moved to the Magny-Cours circuit.

The circuit known as Dijon-Prenois (1974, 1977, 1979, 1981, 1984) is located in Prenois, near Dijon, and was also used during the 1970s and 1980s for

Better known for the famous 24-hour race, the Le Mans circuit held the French Formula One Grand Prix just once in 1967. Here, smoke pours off the wheels as tyres try desperately to grip the road. Graham Hill (number 7 in a Lotus 49-Ford Cosworth), Jack Brabham (number 3 in a Brabham BT24-Repco), and Dan Gurney (number 9 in an Eagle T1G-Weslake) lead the way off the start/finish line.

the French Formula One Grand Prix. Strangely enough, it was used once for the 1982 Swiss Grand Prix – motor racing is banned in Switzerland! The first of these races was run in 1974, initially on the 3.2 km (2 mile) track. Being so short, there was a congestion problem with back-markers, and so in 1975 the track was modified and extended to 3.8 km (2.361 miles). The Grand Prix returned in 1977 and continued there, on and off, until 1984, when

Niki Lauda won the last race in his McLaren TAG. Although the circuit is still used, the Formula One circus has not returned.

The Circuit de la Sarthe (1967), located near Le Mans, is not a permanent track and is most famous for hosting the annual 24-hour of Le Mans race. The track uses local roads that are accessible to the general public for the rest of the year. In 1965 a smaller but permanent Bugatti circuit was added, which shared the pit lane facilities and the first corner (including the famous Dunlop bridge) with its longer track.

For only one year, in 1967, the French Grand Prix was held, to many people's dismay, at the Bugatti circuit at Le Mans. This was not the most popular of choices and only about 20,000 spectators turned up for the event. Still, the drivers turned up and Graham Hill in his Lotus took pole position, with current World Champion Jack Brabham on one side, and

The circuit at Reims was a spectacular triangular road course, using public roads that ran between the villages of Thillois & Gueux. Long fast straights were a great feature of the track, as can be seen here in the 1961 event, where Giancarlo Baghetti (Ferrari Dino 156) leads Dan Gurney (Porsche 718) and Jo Bonnier (number 10 – Porsche 718) under the famous Dunlop bridge. Baghetti and Gurney finished in 1st and 2nd position respectively.

Dan Gurney in his Eagle-Weslake on the other. Although Hill got off to a great start, two Brabhams finished first and second, with Jack Brabham winning the race in his Brabham-Repco BT24.

Reims-Gueux (1950, 1951, 1953, 1954, 1956, 1958-1961, 1963, 1966), was a triangular road course in Reims, northern France, and hosted fourteen French Grand Prix races.

The track was first established in 1925, on the public roads between the small villages of Thillois and Gueux, and included two very long straights between the towns. High speed was the order of the day, and the race organizers even arranged for the

Due to its long fast straights, the Reims circuit often saw races being decided by slipstreaming battles. To obtain even greater speeds, the organizers cut down trees and demolished houses to ease the severity of the corners. Here, in the 1950 event, Giuseppe Farina leads Juan Manuel Fangio and Luigi Fagioli (all driving Alfa Romeo 158) past the grandstands.

By the time the Formula One circus came to Reims in 1952, some major work had been done to the circuit. The pit area had been extended, the track widened and new grandstands had been built. The circuit was run on public roads and had medium straights, a cobbled hairpin bend and some pretty scary bends that worked their way through the wooded countryside. All in all, five Formula One races were held here: the first in 1952, won by Alberto Ascari in a Ferrari, and the last in a rainy 1968, when Jacky Ickx, also in a Ferrari, took the honours ahead of the legendary John Surtees in his Honda.

Many have said, and still do, that the Rouen circuit is the best French circuit of them all. Certainly it had character with its twists and turns through the undulating wooded terrain. Seen here in 1968 is Denny Hulme (McLaren M7A Ford) leading John Surtees (Honda RA301) and Bruce McLaren (McLaren M7A Ford) at the head of the chasing pack.

removal of trees and old houses in order to make the circuit even quicker.

The first official Formula One event at the circuit took place in 1950, and the last Formula One race was held here in 1966. It was in 1952, when the circuit was significantly altered to bypass the village of Gueux, that it was simply referred to as Reims by many people. The circuit was closed permanently in 1972 due to financial difficulties.

Located just three miles south of the town of Rouen is the circuit known as Rouen-les-Essarts (1952, 1957, 1962, 1964, 1968), which many agree used to be one of the finest racing circuits in Europe. The fatal crash sustained by Swiss driver Jo Schlesser in 1968, competing in his first Formula One Grand Prix, hastened the demise of the circuit. Schlesser's Honda engine cut out just prior to the Six Frères bend, and the car slid into the banking, turned over and trapped him. The marshals ran to the scene but the car burst into flames with Schlesser trapped.

The 4.065 mile-long circuit was opened in 1950, and in 1964 Jack Brabham, in a Brabham BT7, clocked the lap record of two minutes, 11.400 seconds, at an average speed of 111.370 mph.

GERMAN GRAND PRIX

Alternating venues: Hockenheimring, Hockenheim, Germany and Nürburgring, Nürburg, Germany

The first place in Germany to stage what was considered a Grand Prix motor racing event was the AVUS (Automobil Verkehrs und Übungs-Straße) race track, located in south-west Berlin. This was in 1926, and the race was won by Rudolf Caracciola, who would go on to make a name for himself with the Mercedes-Benz team. An unfortunate accident, which killed three people, put a stop to further Grand Prix events being staged at the AVUS circuit, although the Grand Prix returned there just once more in 1959. Following this tragic event, the race was moved to the new 28 km-long Nürburgring, which was inaugurated in 1927. The race remained here until the 1970s, when safety concerns once again required it to move, this time to the modern Hockenheimring.

The Nürburgring had several track configurations, but it is only the shorter 1980s version that is currently used for major international racing events. The older and much longer version of the circuit, the Nordschleife (Northern Loop) was built in the 1920s, and went around the village and medieval castle of Nürburg in the beautiful Eifel Mountains. Well-known racing driver Jackie Stewart gave it the nickname 'The Green Hell', as it commanded great respect and was rated one of the most, if not *the* most, demanding purpose-built race tracks in the world.

The track was designed by the Eichler Architekturbüro of Ravensburg, led by architect Gustav Eichler, and construction was started in September 1925. The 'Ring', as it is so often referred to, was 28,265 km (17.5 miles) long and incorporated some 174 bends. It could be split into two sections: the Südschleife (southern loop) of

ENGLAND

NETHERLANDS GERMANY POLAND

BELGIUM NÜRBURGRING

FRANCE CZECH REP

HOCKENHEIMRING

SWITZERLAND AUSTRIA

EINFARHT PARABOLICA

NORD KURVE

2

3

4

HOCHGESCHWINDIGKEITS KURVE

SACHS KURVE

13

START/FINISH

PITS

14

15

5

9

16

10

MERCEDES ARENA

8

SUD KURVE

17

11

7

6

12

MOBIL KURVE

SPITZKEHRE

Hockenheimring, Germany

A view of the pit area at the Hockenheimring circuit, taken during the 2006 Grand Prix. Once a much longer and more interesting circuit that took in the countryside, today it is merely a grand stadium. It does give good spectator viewing, though, and has excellent facilities.

GERMAN GRAND PRIX

7.747 km (4.8 miles) and the Nordschleife of
22.810 km (14 miles), with a shorter circuit
of 2.29 km (1.4 miles) around the pit area being
used on occasion for practice and local events.
As mentioned, the first German Grand Prix at the
circuit was held in 1927, while the circuit was also

Jackie Stewart nicknamed the Nürburgring 'The Green Hell'. It is widely considered the toughest and most demanding purpose-built circuit in the world. Seen here at the 1967 German Grand Prix is the BRM P83 of Stewart, who has just passed the start/finish line and is about to get stuck into the Sudkehre on the Nordschleife circuit.

A rather unenthusiastic Richard 'Dick' Seaman (at the time driving for the Mercedes-Benz team in a model W154) gives a half-hearted Nazi salute after winning the race at the Nürburgring in 1938. Next to him is Major Adolf Hühnlein, a Nazi Party official and Korpsführer of the National Socialist Motor Corps (NSKK), who presented the trophies at German Grand Prix races and made certain that Nazi flags and bunting covered the victory tribunes.

Nürburgring, Germany

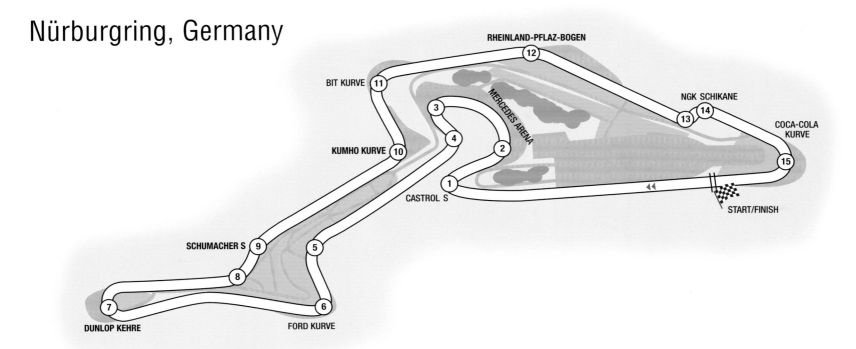

RHEINLAND-PFLAZ-BOGEN

12

BIT KURVE 11

NGK SCHIKANE

13 14

COCA-COLA
KURVE

3

MERCEDES ARENA

4

KUMHO KURVE 10

2

15

1

CASTROL S

START/FINISH

SCHUMACHER S 9

5

8

7 6

DUNLOP KEHRE FORD KURVE

used as a one-way toll road during non-race evenings and weekends. The last time the 'Ring' was used in full was in 1929, after which the Nordschleife was generally used. In the late 1930s a new track was in the process of being built near Dresden. This was called the Deutschlandring, and was due to hold the 1940 Grand Prix. Unfortunately, because of the Second World War, it never happened. After the war, German drivers were banned from participating in international events until 1951. This saw them and their circuits missing the inaugural Formula One season of 1950.

By 1959 Mercedes had decided to pull out of Grand Prix racing and Juan Manuel Fangio, rated as the greatest driver ever, had retired. Suddenly attendance figures started to drop. That year it was decided to host the Grand Prix back at the AVUS circuit, but again the safety problem came up after several accidents, as did the extremely high speeds that were being attained. Owing to the new rules that would be imposed on Formula One cars for 1961, a Formula Two race was held here in 1960. This saw Joakim Bonnier finish first in a Porsche

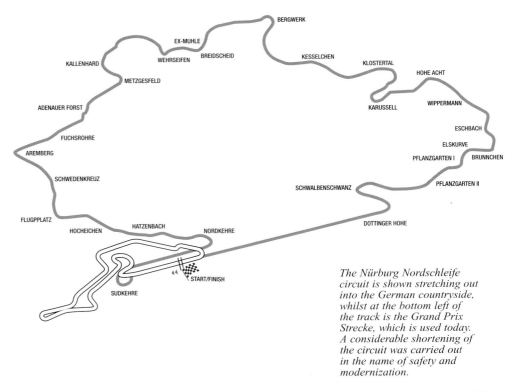

The Nürburg Nordschleife circuit is shown stretching out into the German countryside, whilst at the bottom left of the track is the Grand Prix Strecke, which is used today. A considerable shortening of the circuit was carried out in the name of safety and modernization.

had been much improved but only hosted the race this one year, although its turn would soon come around again. The race returned to the Nordschleife track, which in the meantime had been much improved. It remained here for a further six years and saw drivers such as Clay Regazzoni, Carlos Reutemann and English playboy James Hunt cross the finish line in first position. The 1976 season started well for Niki Lauda and the Ferrari team. He won four of the first six races and came second in the other two, so points were amassing rapidly for a second championship. More points came in the

718. (The race was run at the shorter Südschleife track.) The following year, 1961, the Grand Prix once again returned to the Nürburgring Nordschleife, where ace British driver Stirling Moss scored a happy victory in his Lotus Climax. The race remained at the Nordschleife circuit up to 1970, when it was moved to the Hockenheimring. (Safety requirements had been requested by the drivers, but not met in time.) During this period, Ferrari, Brabham, Lotus, BRM and even a Matra took the checkered flag in first place. Graham Hill, John Surtees, Jim Clark, Jack Brabham, Denny Hulme, Jackie Stewart and Jackie Ickx, all household names by now, were winners at the circuit. Hockenheim

In 1959 the AVUS circuit hosted its only world championship Formula One German Grand Prix. Sadly the weekend also saw the death of Jean Behra, when his Porsche flew over the top of the North Turn banking. The result was a 1,2,3 for the Ferrari team, with Tony Brooks taking the honours in his Dino 246. Here Brooks leads Stirling Moss and Masten Gregory on the North Turn.

Minutes prior to the start of the 1967 German Grand Prix at the Nürburgring: Jim Clark (Lotus 49 Ford), Denny Hulme (Brabham BT24 Repco), Jackie Stewart (BRM P155) and Dan Gurney (Eagle T1G Weslake) are on the front row of the grid.

The 1957 German Grand Prix was held at the Nürburgring. Juan Manuel Fangio, seen here, overcame a considerable gap between himself and the leaders to win the race and the 1957 Word Championship in what many, including Fangio himself, consider his greatest performance. It was also rated as the single greatest drive in auto racing history by the editors of Motorsport magazine.

Not a bad view of the Nürburgring: Nordschleif circuit during the 1972 German Grand Prix and away from the main grandstand and pit area. The cars are seen racing up the incline that leads from the Klostertal into a sharp right and then into the Karssell hairpin, before going on to the Hohe Acht right-hand bend.

British Grand Prix and so when he got to Germany he had nearly double the points of his closest rival Jody Scheckter – a second world title seemed a formality. Germany though was to bring him bad luck, and even today doctors do not understand how he survived. On the second lap of the race, his car swerved off the track, hit the embankment and rolled back on to the oncoming car of Brett Lunger. The car burst into flames, trapping Lauda in the cockpit. Arturo Merzario, Guy Edwards and Lunger tried to free him from the wreckage but the damage was done. He suffered incredible burns to his head and inhaled toxic fumes, which also damaged his lungs and contaminated his blood. Somehow they managed to get him out of the car in a conscious state, but he was later to fall into a coma and was even administered the last rites. The man spent time in hospital and recovered to drive again . . . that very season. Had it not been for an extraordinarily wet Japanese Grand Prix, which Lauda felt he was unable to drive in, he would without doubt have won his second championship. Instead, James Hunt went on to clinch it by a single point. Lauda is a regular visitor to the race circuits of the world and is still seen with his famous cap, which is not only a trademark but helps to hide the terrible scars he incurred. This accident was instrumental in moving the race back to the Hockenheimring in 1977, which has been its permanent home, except for 1985 when it was run at the new 4.5 km (2.8 miles) Nürburgring circuit. The Nürburgring circuit continues to be used, particularly for the Formula

This is a great aerial view of the new Nürburgring, which has been refurbished by Herman Tilke and his German company.

Just like the Nürburgring, Hockenheim was also a much longer circuit before it was reduced in size and became the motordrome it is today. Niki Lauda is seen in his Ferrari 312T2 in 1977 on his way to another victory – and eventually another World Championship.

The start of the 2001 German Grand Prix at Hockenheim: Luciano Burti is seen flying through the air. With cars jostling for position, Burti had not seen the slow car of Michael Schumacher and ploughed straight into the back of it, somersaulting and skidding down the track, ending up in the gravel trap on the Nord Kurve. Fortunately no one was hurt or killed.

One European Grand Prix, which was held there on a regular basis up to 2007 – when it was announced that it would be removed from the calendar for 2008, after which the two circuits would take it in turn to host the official German Grand Prix.

The Hockenheim race circuit (Hockenheimring), situated outside the small town of the same name, has become not only one of the most modern race tracks, but is also overflowing with history.

In 1930 a young assistant timekeeper, Ernst Christ, presented an idea for a race circuit to be built in the town. The mayor, Philipp Klein, supported the idea and just a year later the plans for the new circuit were approved by the local council. Building began at the beginning of 1932 and just two months later, on 25 May, the first motorcycle race was run on the new track. By 1938 the circuit was due for change, but the basic layout was used up to 2001, with the inclusion of the Ostkurve and a general widening of the track. The Second World War temporarily stopped racing and the track was also badly damaged during this time. Repairs took place after the war and by 1947 cars and motorcycles were once again seen circulating the track.

During the 1960s, with the construction of the main Mannheim to Walldorf motorway planned to cut through the circuit, it had to be changed. It was now that Ernst Christ came up with the Motodrom idea, and with a handsome compensation payment work began in 1964. By 1966 the new Motodrom was in full use. Two tragic dates must be mentioned: in 1968 Jim Clark was killed in a Formula 2 race,

Taken prior to the start of the 1970 German Grand Prix at Hockenheim, this view shows the activity on the start-line. Jacky Ickx (Ferrari 312B), Jochen Rindt (Lotus 72C Ford), Clay Regazzoni (Ferrari 312B), Jo Siffert (March 701-Ford), Henri Pescarolo (Matra-Simca MS120) and Chris Amon (March 701 Ford) line up on the grid.

and 1980 saw Patrick Depailler also killed there. Changes occurred after both these fatalities. It was in 1970 that the first official Formula One race was held there, and more than 100,000 spectators gathered to watch Jochen Rindt take the checkered flag in his Lotus-Ford. The race moved away until 1977, when Niki Lauda took the checkered flag on his way to a second World Championship. The original circuit was quite long and ran into hilly, wooded areas, which were difficult for spectators to get to and which were also considered a danger to the drivers. It was therefore decided to shorten the track and bring it slap up to date, the work being given to the design company of Hermann Tilke. No stranger to Formula One circuit design, he went to work and shortened the track considerably and cut

The 2006 German Grand Prix saw the two Ferrari drivers, Michael Schumacher and Felipe Massa, take first and second place respectively. Here, Ferrari fans swarm towards the winners' podium to see and congratulate their heroes.

Nothing like a little light entertainment! Giving a carnival feel to the proceedings, these performers are happy to keep the crowds amused in their somewhat skimpy but beautiful outfits.

A dangerous moment at the 1994 Grand Prix at Hockenheim after Jos Verstappen had come in for his pit-stop. As the refueller pulled the fuel hose away, the valve stuck open, allowing fuel to continue flowing over the car. This ignited into a huge fireball that engulfed Benetton mechanic Paul Seaby. Thankfully, no one was seriously injured in the dramatic incident.

out the forest section. This was not a popular move but certainly made it more user-friendly, more compact, and safer.

It now has a capacity of 120,000 due to large new grandstands sponsored by Mercedes-Benz, and the complex also features a quarter-mile track for drag racing. Come to Hockenheim even when there is nothing on, as there is a motorsport museum and you can even drive the circuit. Hockenheim is some 90 km (56 miles) away from the international Frankfurt Am Main Airport, with the A5 road link being the most convenient to use when coming from Frankfurt. Train services are excellent and there is even a hotel on the circuit, but check it out before you get there as it can be very booked up on race days.

CZECH REP

SLOVAKIA
UKRAINE

AUSTRIA

● HUNGARORING

HUNGARY

ROMANIA

CROATIA

BOSNIA-
HERZEGOVINA   SERBIA

HUNGARIAN GRAND PRIX

Venue: Hungaroring, Mogyorod, Hungary

The Hungaroring Formula One race circuit is located near Budapest in Hungary, and is the venue used for the Hungarian Grand Prix. When first staged there in 1986, it became the first Formula One Grand Prix to be held behind the Iron Curtain. Bernie Ecclestone – president of FOA (previously FOCA) – was keen to have a Grand Prix in the USSR, but it seems that a friend recommended he contact Budapest. The original idea was to have a city-centre circuit at Népliget – Budapest's biggest park – on the same lines as Monaco. The then communist government had different ideas, though, and built a whole new track just outside the city beside a major motorway. The building of the track broke all records – it took a mere eight months to finish – and the race is still run there today, some twenty years later, and with that record still intact.

The first Hungarian Grand Prix dates back to 1936, when in June of that year, on a circuit in the centre of Népliget, Budapest, cars were assembled to do battle with the all-conquering Mercedes and Auto-Union racing teams. Alfa-Romeo and Maserati sent teams, and even a Ford V8 was entered by Petre Cristea, a Romanian driver who also won the Monte Carlo Rally that year. Famous

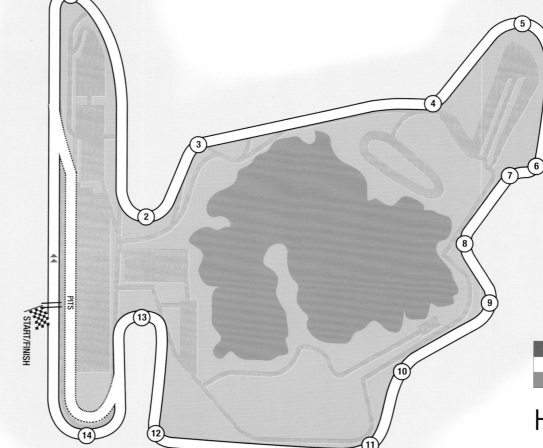

Hungaroring, Hungary

The 2005 Hungarian Grand Prix saw the beginning of the end of tobacco advertising in Formula One. McLaren (West) and B·A·R (Lucky Strike) ran with tobacco livery before withdrawing it for the race. Ferrari (Marlboro) and Renault (Mild Seven) ran full tobacco livery for the entire weekend. Here, Kimi Raikkonen in his McLaren Mercedes MP4-20 crosses the line to take victory.

A scene from the first Hungarian Grand Prix of 1936 shows one of the all-conquering Auto-Unions, driven by Hans Stuck, negotiating one of the corners at the Nepliget Park circuit.

The Hungaroring is situated in a valley surrounded by fifty hectares of rolling hillside. With this exceptional location, almost eighty percent of the racetrack is visible from nearly any point – a great plus for spectators. Here, the cars are seen at the start of the 1986 race, headed by Nelson Piquet in a Williams FW11 Honda.

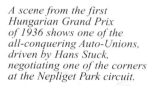

drivers of the period were there – Bernd Rosemeyer, Hans Stuck, Manfred von Brauchitsch, Rudolf Caracciola and of course Tazio Nuvolari. To the surprise of many, Nuvolari, driving an Alfa, took the checkered flag in first position, after the Mercedes and Auto-Union cars experienced problems. It is quite amazing to think that 100,000 people turned up to see the race, a large number of spectators for the period and venue. By this time, though, war clouds were massing and with the political situation being what it was, Grand Prix racing came to a halt in Hungary as in many other countries in Europe.

It wasn't until 1986 that the next Grand Prix would be run in Hungary, which would also be the first in the Formula One category in that country.

The Hungaroring is situated 19 km from the centre of Budapest, and borders the village of Mogyoród on the M3 motorway. The circuit lies in a natural valley and is surrounded by rolling hills, and there is excellent viewing from nearly any position around the track. The original length of the circuit was 4.014 km (2.49 miles), but after a change to an 'S' bend combination in 1989, it was reduced to 3.971 km (2.467 miles). Further construction work carried out in 2003 meant that the start/finish straight was lengthened by 20 metres (approx. 663 feet),

The start/finish straight of the Hungaroring is the fastest part of the circuit and although it is one of the safest tracks on the race calendar, it is also considered to be one of the least exciting. The 2003 race was dismal for the Ferrari team. Here, Rubens Barrichello leads the chasing pack.

The 2005 Hungarian Grand Prix was full of mishaps, but the most spectacular was when Christian Klien made contact with Jacques Villeneuve. Their wheels touched as they fought for position at turn 1, sending Klien into a spectacular barrel-roll before he finished the right way up. Fortunately, he was unharmed.

changing the length of the track to 4.381 km
(2.72 miles). The average race length is 306.66 km
(190.55 miles) over seventy laps. The circuit is
considered one of the safest on the calendar and
for this reason is often seen as boring, especially as
there aren't too many overtaking points. It is a twisty
track and can often be 'dirty' with dust, debris and
rubbish accumulating from its infrequent use during
the rest of the year. The race is held in the middle of
the European summer and temperatures can be high
and uncomfortable, with the breeze whipping up
dust and dirt on to the track. Having said this,
though, there have been some memorable moments
and the race is very popular not only with the home
crowd, but also with neighbouring Germany and
with the Finnish fans, some of whom share the
common Finno-Ugric languages. With little chance
of overtaking, races are generally won either with a
good position on the starting grid or with pit-stop
strategy. That is unless you are Nigel Mansell of
course, who during the 1989 race managed to take
himself from twelfth on the grid to finish the race in
first place. Schumacher and Ferrari are experts when
it comes to pit strategy and this was shown in 1998,
when the team changed its strategy halfway through

*All hands to the pumps!
A view of a modern-day
pit-stop, carried out with
military precision by the
masters, Ferrari. Mika
Häkkinen's gearbox problem
allowed Michael Schumacher
to win the 1998 race after
using a three-stop strategy.
This was seen as a masterstroke
by tactician Ross Brawn.*

*The 2006 Hungarian Grand
Prix was an incident-packed
thriller which saw Jenson
Button, pictured, win his first
Formula One race despite
starting down in 14th position.
The track was wet at the start of
the race, making it the first-ever
wet Hungarian Grand Prix.*

The wet start of the seventy-lap, 2006 Hungarian Grand Prix: polesitter Kimi Räikkönen races ahead of his rivals to take an early lead, his McLaren team-mate Pedro de la Rosa tucking in behind.

These Ferrari fans celebrate after the team of Schumacher and Barrichello dominated the weekend. Hungary is a hop from Germany and so there is no lack of support for Schumacher and his Ferrari team.

the race and Schumacher put in one of his best-ever drives to build up a winning margin, giving him the race win. Several drivers have had their first Grand Prix wins at the circuit too: Damon Hill in 1993, Fernando Alonso in 2003 and more recently, Jenson Button in 2006, in the first wet Hungarian Grand Prix race.

Along with the Grand Prix the circuit also offers open days for cars, a racing school and an adventure park. There is also a karting circuit nearby and a technical driving centre.

Budapest, just a hop away and the eighth largest city in the European Union, has approximately 1.7 million inhabitants and is a single city occupying both banks of the river Danube. The city has charm and intrigue and a visit there is a must before you return home.

TURKISH GRAND PRIX

Venue: Istanbul Park, Tuzla/Istanbul, Turkey

The Formula One race circuit of Istanbul Park became a project of national importance for the Republic of Turkey, with the first race scheduled for the 2005 Formula One season. The circuit is located on the Asian side of Istanbul 6 km from the junction of Kurtkoy on the north side of TEM Motorway which links Istanbul to Ankara. The site is close to, and has good access to and from, the Sabiha Gokcen Istanbul Airport. It is surrounded by a forest and agricultural fields.

This is another of the few tracks that run in an anti-clockwise direction. It is 5.333 km (3.315 miles) in length and has an average track width of 14–21.5 metres (45.931–70.53 feet), not including the run-off areas. All in all there are fourteen corners – six right and eight left – the sharpest of which has a radius of 15 metres (49.212 feet), with the start/finish straight being 655.5 metres (2150.6 feet) long.

The main Grand Stand can seat 26,250 spectators, and along with the temporary grand stands and general admission areas provided, a total capacity of over 130,000 spectators is catered for.

Once again this is a Tilke-designed circuit, and he has made a point of following the undulations of the local terrain, somewhat in contrast to some of his other designs. It is influenced by other circuits in the Formula One calendar – corner 1 for example is very similar to corner 1 at the Autódromo José Carlos Pace in Brazil, and has also been

Istanbul Park, Turkey

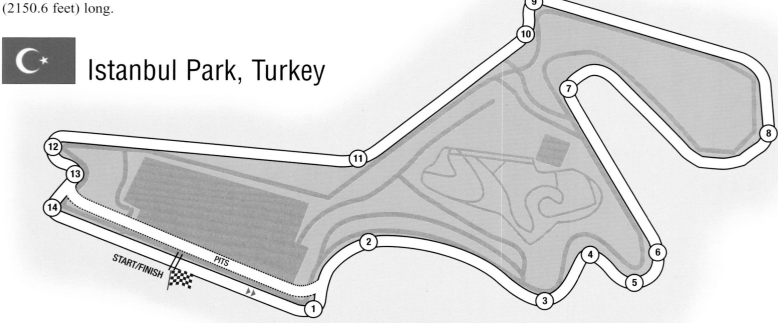

A pit lane scene taken during Friday practice for the 2005 Turkish Grand Prix, as mechanics and technicians prepare the cars for their drivers. Formula One has certainly come a long way since the early days!

TURKISH GRAND PRIX

compared to the 'corkscrew' at Laguna Seca. Turn 8 can be an exciting corner for both spectator and driver. It is long, tight, has a 'G' force factor of 5 – five times the force of gravity – and lasts for a full four seconds. It takes a very fit person to endure this kind of pressure, lap after lap. One driver who did slip up here was Juan Pablo Montoya, who was comfortably positioned in second place on the penultimate lap of the 2005 race. When he braked too hard after overtaking the lapped Jordan of Tiago Monteiro, contact was made and the damage sustained caused Montoya to lose grip on the rear of the car on the next lap, forcing him to run straight on at turn 8. The result was the loss of second position to Fernando Alonso and a possible first

The teams are making all the last necessary checks as the drivers sit calmly contemplating their first corner. This is the scene on the grid of the 2006 Turkish Grand Prix.

The start/finish line is a long way off, but spectators still have an incredible view from the grandstands. Giancarlo Fisichella (Renault R25) leads Kimi Raikkonen (McLaren Mercedes MP4-20), Fernando Alonso (Renault R25) and Juan Pablo Montoya (McLaren Mercedes MP4-20), among others, around turn 1 at the start of the 2005 race.

The Istanbul Park circuit has been likened in several places to other circuits, and is generally appreciated by the drivers. Sharp bends mix with fast straights to catch the driver out. Here Tiago Monteiro (Jordan Toyota EJ15) is hounded by Christian Klien at the 2005 Turkish Grand Prix.

As if keeping the car on the road wasn't hard enough, blind hilltops create great difficulties for the driver when judging the next bend. Here Ralf Schumacher (Toyota TF106B) leads Mark Webber (Williams FW28-Cosworth) over the brow of the hill in the 2006 Turkish Grand Prix.

championship for Montoya. The race was eventually won by Kimi Räikkönen in his McLaren Mercedes.

There were some complaints that the circuit got bumpier as the weekend progressed, a similar criticism to that aimed at the Shanghai circuit.

Turkey held its last Formula One race in 2011, after which it was dropped from the race calendar and looks unlikely to regain a spot in the near future due to finances and competition from other nations in the Formula One global line-up.

Other events held at the circuit include the MotoGP series, FIA World Touring Car Championship, GP2, Formula-G, Deutsche Tourenwagen Masters and the Le Mans Series 1000 km (621 miles) race.

ITALIAN GRAND PRIX

Venue: Autodromo Nazionale di Monza, Parco di Monza, Milan, Italy

The Monza circuit, just outside Milan in northern Italy, hosts the Italian Formula One Grand Prix. It is notable for the fact that, due to its long straights, drivers are on full throttle for a higher-than-average percentage of the lap. It is a flat circuit with little variation in elevation, and is regarded as a track which tests horsepower rather than driver skill – one of those circuits where the phrase 'no guts no glory' comes to mind. The Italian Grand Prix was one of the inaugural Formula One championship races in 1950, and has been held every year since then. The circuit has great facilities and is a very popular race venue, in particular during the Grand Prix. Monza park is a delight and it is a hop away from Milan with all its shopping possibilities and wonderful restaurants.

Besides being a major international sporting event of the post-war period, the first Italian Grand Prix was also of great technical significance. The combustion engine had developed impressively during the war period, and therefore post-war races were more than just competitions between drivers. They were also an opportunity for the racing nations to demonstrate, in front of adoring crowds, their technical know-how.

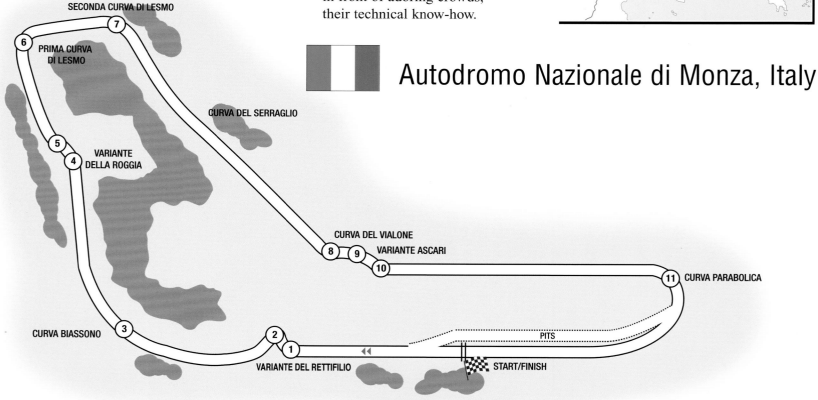

Autodromo Nazionale di Monza, Italy

This photo, taken during the 1996 Italian Grand Prix at Monza, shows just how beautiful the surrounding area is. Here, Jean Alesi in his Benetton B196 Renault is shown at the exit of Parabolica and about to enter the start/finish straight.

This first race, on 4 September 1921, was not run at the Monza circuit – which was still to be built – but took place at the triangular-configured track at Montichiari, near the town of Brescia, in northern Italy. Of the twenty expected entrants, only six turned up: three Fiat cars, driven by Wagner, Sivocci and Bordino, and three Ballot cars, driven by Di Palma, Chassagne and Goux. The last mentioned finally went on to win the race, and at an average speed of 144 kph (90 mph).

Following such an exceptional first race, it was seen by the different Italian manufacturers as very important that they should have a fixed place to test their vehicles. The Milan Automobile Club was also instrumental in forcing this idea through; the building of a circuit would also be a celebration of their twenty-fifth anniversary. The initial choices for the circuit were the 'moorland' area of Gallerate, where Malpensa airport lies today, and the Cagnola

The new Monza circuit was built in only 110 days. This scene shows some of the workers cutting down trees and preparing the ground. In the corner of the picture the narrow-gauge railway engine can be seen at full steam.

district on the outskirts of Milan. Finally, though, a decision was taken to build it at the Villa Reale Park, Monza, Milan. The architect was Alfredo Rosselli and the board chairman was Senator Silvio Crespi. The first stone was laid by Vincenzo Lancia and Felice Nazzaro, and although some objections were motioned, adjustments to the layout and its size were carried out and building resumed. There are some incredible statistics to be mentioned regarding the building of the autodrome: it was built in 110 days using 3,500 workers, 200 wagons, thirty lorries and a narrow gauge railway – 5 km (3 miles) long – running two locos and eighty cars. Petro Bordino

The new Monza circuit was officially opened on a rainy 3 September 1922, with a Voiturette race being held and won by Pietro Bordino in a racing model Fiat 501. A week later on 10 September, the second Italian Grand Prix was again won by Bordino, but this time in a 6-cylinder Fiat 804.

and Felice Nazzaro drove the full circuit on 28 July 1922 in a Fiat 570. The track consisted of a high-speed loop with a total length of 4.5 km (2.79 miles), and featured two banked corners which rose 2.6 metres (8.5 feet) above ground level. The banked corners contributed to a possible top speed of between 180–190 kph (112–118 mph), and were joined by two straights 1,070 metres (3,242 feet) long. The road track was 5.5 km (3.41 miles) long and again the two straights were connected on the south by the 'little curve', which was also slightly banked. These two tracks intersected at two levels and had an underpass at the Serraglio area.

Nuvolari was only a very small man and it is incredible to think that he was able to throw one of these huge Auto-Union D racing machines around with skill and precision. Here he is seen negotiating one of the sharp bends at the 1938 Grand Prix of Monza, which he went on to win.

The driver Bordino pictured in his Fiat. Here he is seen about to overtake the Bugatti 30 of De Vizcaya at the Milan Grand Prix of the Automobile Club of Italy. 1922 saw both a voiturette race and the second Italian Grand Prix at the new Monza circuit.

Circuito di Milano Gran Premio dell' A. C. d'Italia
BORDINO sorpassa la Bugatti

ITALIAN GRAND PRIX

The first race to take place at the new Monza circuit was seen as a return duel between the Italian and French racing teams. Thirty-eight entrants were listed for the race but sadly only ten turned up. Of these, the two Austro-Daimler cars retired after the fatal crash of their German colleague Kuhn. Of all the cars present, it was the Bugattis that proved the only real competitors to the Fiat team. Some 150,000 people turned up to see this race, an incredible number of spectators. It was run with little incident and at the end it was Bordino in a six-cylinder Fiat 804 who won, followed in by Nazzaro and finally De Vizcaya in his Bugatti. And so for the following years, as for this race, the competition was run on the full 10 km (6.25 mile) circuit. Within a few years, though, cars began to

During the Second World War the Monza circuit was badly damaged. Much rebuilding and refurbishment was carried out, as can be seen in this picture. The 1949 race was won by Alberto Ascari in a Ferrari 125. He is seen here on the futuristic new podium.

get considerably faster as superchargers and other speed enhancing changes were incorporated. For example, by 1924 and 1925 the very fast, supercharged Alfa Romeo P2s were reaching speeds of over 220 kph (136 mph), and were dangerously close to exceeding the limits that had been calculated for the banking. It was 1928 when the Italian Grand Prix suffered its worst accident to date, with Emilio Materassi involved in a collision on the grandstand straight: he died along with twenty-seven spectators. Following this, the race was run solely on the high-speed loop for safety reasons. All the same, Varzi and Alfieri Maserati, driving Maseratis,

managed to reach 200 kph (124 mph) for the first time. During this period, Vincenzo Florio, president of the Automobile Sports Commission, had studied a new course which left the structure of the circuit unchanged but made use of the road circuit and banked corner on the south side, linked by a short straight and two ninety-degree bends. This became known as the Florio circuit and was 6,680 metres (4.14 miles) in length. The race returned to the 10 km circuit in 1932 and 1933, when three fatal accidents happened, killing Campari, Borzacchini and Czaykowski. With so many deaths, other layouts were tried, with artificial chicanes and sharp bends being incorporated to slow the cars down. Racing returned briefly to the Florio circuit, before being run at Livorno in 1937. It then returned to the Florio circuit in 1938, where Tazio Nuvolari in an Auto-Union beat the all-conquering Mercedes team. The year 1938 saw a major overhaul of the circuit and its buildings. The road circuit was resurfaced, the two banked curves were demolished on the high-speed

Spectators and photographers alike wait for the man to lower his flag for the start of the 1957 Italian Grand Prix at Monza. The all-Vanwall line-up is spoilt by Fangio on the right in his Maserati. Number 22 is the car of Stirling Moss, who also beat Fangio across the winning line.

By the late 1960s Monza had become an extremely fast circuit, with the cars now equipped with all kinds of aerodynamic features. It also became highly dangerous. This is Graham Hill in a Lotus 49B Ford with additional rear wing at the 1968 race. Note also the spectators in the trees behind!

track, a new and larger concrete central grandstand was erected, new pits and service buildings were built, and a new scoreboard was put up for the public. All racing stopped during the Second World War and the circuit fell into disrepair. However, in 1948 it was refurbished by the Milan Automobile Club. Major car racing events were staged at the Valentino circuit in Milan during this year, but later that same year there was an Autodrome Grand Prix at the new circuit in Monza. With all its new facilities, the circuit now hosted all the events between 1949 and 1954, with more improvements happening along the way. In 1955 work began to entirely revamp the circuit, which would result in a 5.75 km (3.6 mile) course including a new 4.25 km (2.7 mile) high-speed oval with banked curves.

This image, taken at Monza in 1965, gives an impression of calm and ease. In fact Jim Clark, Jackie Stewart, Graham Hill and Dan Gurney are judging their drift around the Parabolica bend with the greatest precision and daring. One false move of the steering wheel and the car could let go, resulting in certain destruction and possible death.

The Italian Grand Prix of 1978: Ronnie Peterson (Lotus 78-Ford) leads Alan Jones (Williams FW06-Ford) and the rest of the field on the race warm-up lap. The actual race was started too early, with cars at the back of the grid still moving, causing a pile-up at the first chicane. Ronnie Peterson, who crashed heavily, died later in hospital.

The 1970 Italian Grand Prix: this was a tragic weekend that saw Jochen Rindt's Lotus crash heavily into the barriers at the Parabolica. Rindt was rushed to hospital but was dead on arrival. Here, spectators watch as eventual winner Clay Regazzoni (Ferrari 312B) brakes hard for the Parabolica.

When combined, the two circuits would also create a 10 km-long circuit, with cars running parallel on the main straight. At the same time, the infrastructure was also upgraded. This high-speed track was used again for the Italian Grand Prix in 1955, 1956, 1960 and finally in 1961, when driver Wolfgang von Trips was fatally injured and eleven spectators lost their lives near the infamous Parabolica curve. Even though the banking was not responsible for the accident, this saw the end of the oval circuit being used for single-seater cars – except of course for the film *Grand Prix*, made in 1966. Further safety measures were now incorporated, which included crash barriers, walls and railings, and in 1965 run-off areas were added to the corners. But Formula One cars were now reaching excessive speeds, due partly to the addition of wide tyres and aerodynamic 'wings'.

More accidents were to follow, with both car and motorcycle drivers dying of their injuries: 1970 saw Jochen Rindt killed during a qualifying session; in 1973 Renzo Pasolini and Jarno Saarinen crashed heavily during the 250cc motorcycle Grand Prix delle Nazioni, and both were killed. That year Carlo Chionio, Renzo Colombini and Renato Galtrucco died during the 500cc Junior Italian motorcycle championship and in 1978 Ronnie Peterson died of his injuries in hospital. Although motor racing was in one of its most dangerous periods, the actual racing was exceptional, with drivers dicing with each other at very high speeds. The 1970 Grand Prix saw Clay Regazzoni, in a Ferrari, pull away from a chasing pack to win the race in the dying moments. Again, in 1971 five cars battled at high speed to dominate the race, with just yards between them. This was the fastest

Michael Schumacher (Ferrari 248F1), winner of the 2006 Italian Grand Prix, talks about his impending retirement from Formula One. Kimi Räikkönen (McLaren MP4/21-Mercedes-Benz), who finished second and was destined to take Schumacher's place at Ferrari in 2007, listens to what is said at the FIA Press Conference.

You could be forgiven for thinking this is a scene from the movie Gladiator! In fact this shows hordes of fans invading the podium area after Michael Schumacher won the 2006 Italian Grand Prix. There is no stopping the fanatical Ferrari tifosi, especially as their hero was about to announce his retirement.

race in Formula One history, and featured the closest finish, with Peter Gethin coming from fourth position to lead on the final lap. Technology continued to improve vehicle speeds and the track was again changed in 1979. Kerbs were added, run-off areas were extended and tyre-barriers were improved, and further safety work along with infrastructure changes, was undertaken throughout the 1980s.

Jody Scheckter won the Grand Prix in 1979, along with the World Championship in a Ferrari. It would be some years before Ferrari would see another World Championship. In 1980, with changes being made to Monza the race was run at the Imola circuit. Turbo-charging was now also being

Although they went through a lean period prior to Schumacher joining the team, they have bounced back in true and gritty form. After winning the 2006 Italian Grand Prix, Michael Schumacher announced his retirement from Formula One racing at the end of the season. Kimi Räikkönen replaced Schumacher for the 2007 season, driving alongside Felipe Massa. This was a formidable pair and although Massa had a start-stop type of season, Kimi went on to win the Drivers Championship that same year.

Besides the Formula One Grand Prix, and its associated test days, Monza also stages other forms of motor racing events along with other non-racing events. Camp sites can be used on a daily basis and there is a swimming pool for those hot days of the year. Monza is a working park and is not just open for the Grand Prix.

A scene from the 2006 Italian Grand Prix: Rubens Barrichello (Honda RA106), Felipe Massa (Ferrari 248 F1) and Jarno Trulli (Toyota TF106) passing the pit area and grandstands at the start/finish line.

Michael Schumacher makes his way towards the Rettifilo during the 1997 Italian Grand Prix. On the right, clearly in view, is the first banked corner of the old Monza circuit.

introduced, and it is interesting to note that when Rene Arnoux took his Renault to victory in 1982, his average speed was 219 kph (136.87 mph). Just a few years later in 1987, Nelson Piquet won the race at an average speed of 232 kph (145 mph). Speeds continued to climb and circuit owners struggled to keep up with the safety requirements. As the eighties turned into the nineties, more and more safety features were introduced to the circuit, along with track widening and infrastructure improvements.

In 2000 the chicane on the main straight was altered, changing from a double left-right chicane, to a single right-left chicane in an attempt to reduce the frequent accidents at the start of the races. The second chicane was also retroflex. Monza has seen some great races but the team to support is obviously Ferrari – this is their home after all.

BELGIAN GRAND PRIX

Venue: Circuit de Spa-Francorchamps, Belgium

There is no doubting that the Circuit de Spa-Francorchamps in Belgium is one of the best circuits on the Formula One calendar. The most famous part of the circuit, and one of the most dangerous parts too, is the Eau Rouge/Raidillon complex of bends. Once you have successfully negotiated La Source, a hairpin turn, then you accelerate as hard as you possibly can, with the need to take Eau Rouge flat out at some 300 kph (187.5 mph), something that all drivers, past and present, have wanted to do! Many have come unstuck, their attempts ending up with an exceptionally heavy side-on crash. As the circuit has been modified through the years though, it is now generally understood that due to the slight straightening and widening of the complex, flat-out is possible and in fact fairly normal.

The Belgian Grand Prix was first held at the Spa circuit in 1924, but it was not the same track that it is today. The original circuit was a triangle and designed by Jules de Their and Henri Langlois van Ophem. Using public roads it was 15 km (9 miles) long and ran between the towns of Francorchamps, Malmédy and Stavelot. Up until

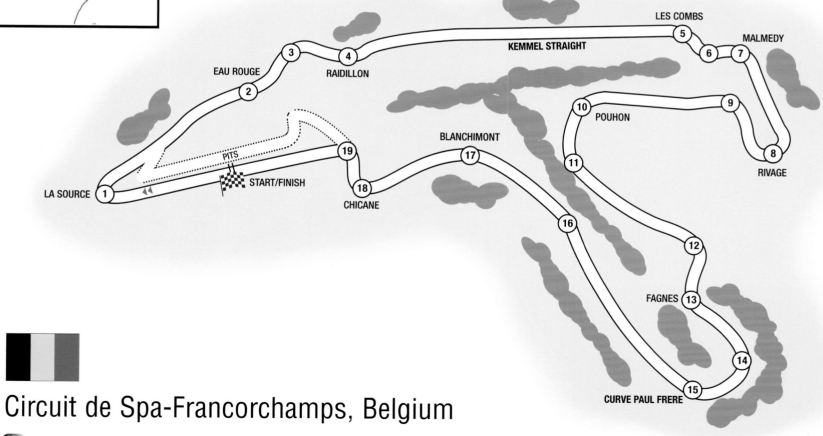

Circuit de Spa-Francorchamps, Belgium

2000 it was still possible to travel over part of the actual race track, as it was part of the public roads.

Belgians loved their racing fast, and to increase the overall speed of the old circuit, they modified the slow uphill 'U-turn' at the bottom of the Eau Rouge creek valley, known as Ancient Douane, by cutting it short and giving it a faster sweep up the

Raidillon hill. The circuit then continued past Les Combes to Bournenville and on towards Malmédy, after which the Masta straight was encountered along with the fast Masta kink, and finally on to Stavelot. A sharp right-hand corner then led you on to another fast straight through the forest to Blanchimont, where the old now meets the new.

This nostalgic scene was taken during a practice session at the 1966 Belgian Grand Prix at Spa-Francorchamps. Although a busy pit lane, most of the activity seems to be from the photographers. The threatening grey skies did unleash rain during the race, which was won by John Surtees in a Ferrari.

BELGIAN GRAND PRIX

The circuit has been modified on several occasions over the years, and today it is 6.9 km (4.3 miles) long. Drivers can reach a staggering 330 kph (206 mph) on parts of the circuit, and the demands on the drivers are enormous. Having said this, it still remains a popular circuit with both drivers and spectators. The Spa race has always been plagued by unpredictable weather and a driver can often find himself in a rain-storm on one part of the circuit, whilst just a few metres down the track the sun is shining. All these unpredictable situations make the racing that much more interesting and exciting.

The first Belgian Grand Prix was won by Antonio Ascari, who was tragically killed in the French Grand Prix, just a few weeks later. His son Alberto went on to win the races in 1952 and 1953. The British racing driver Richard 'Dick' Seaman was tragically killed at the circuit in 1939 whilst leading the race, and during the 1960 race Chris Bristow and Alan Stacey lost their lives in separate incidents – the latter when a bird hit him in the face.

By 1972 the circuit was deemed to be too dangerous for Formula One cars, which by now were becoming extremely fast. It has to be remembered that safety precautions were nowhere near what they

A photograph taken during the Saturday qualifying session of the 2005 Grand Prix: David Coulthard (Red Bull Racing Cosworth RB1) heads towards Eau Rouge. The start/finish line and pits can be easily spotted in the background.

circuit as a Formula One venue, even though the track itself was not seen as being at fault for Villeneuve's death.

The other circuit, Nivelles-Baulers (or Nivelles as most people called it), was 3.7 km (2.314 miles) long and located near Brussels in Belgium. This was built in 1971and designed to be a safer alternative to the Spa circuit. Due to the safety features incorporated, many described it as bland and sterile with rather boring racing. Spectators didn't take to it, saying that they couldn't get close enough to the action. Although the two circuits were intended to stage the Grand Prix in turn, Nivelles

A view of the 1964 Belgian Grand Prix at Spa: Giancarlo Baghetti, driving a BRM P57, leads a group of cars at Radillon, having left Eau Rouge in the distance.

Oh to be a cameraman! One slip by Jack Brabham in his Brabham BT19-Repco and there would have been an awful accident. Getting close to the action is one thing, but this is definitely a little dangerous! This is the Belgian Grand Prix of 1966 at Spa.

are today! So the race was staged at two other venues, each putting the event on in alternate years. The Zolder circuit, also known as Circuit Terlaemen, is 3,977 km (2.622 miles) in length, and is situated at Heusden-Zolder, Belgium. It was built in 1963 and hosted the Grand Prix on ten occasions during the 1970s and 1980s. The first race was hosted here in 1973, and saw Jackie Stewart winning in his Tyrrell-Ford. Niki Lauda, driving a Ferrari, took the chequered flag in both the next two Grand Prix to be staged here in 1975 and 1976, with Michele Alboreto, also driving a Ferrari, winning the last race in 1984.

Unfortunately the circuit has become infamous for the dreadful accident in which Gilles Villeneuve lost his life in 1982, and many people still tend to associate the circuit with that event. It was also this tragic incident that signalled the decline of the

BELGIAN GRAND PRIX

only actually held it twice. In 1972 the race was won by Emerson Fittipaldi in a McLaren-Ford, and in 1974 he won again but this time in a Lotus-Ford. The circuit hit problems early on, with the organizers going bankrupt after the 1974 race. Then in 1976 it was seen as too dangerous to hold the Grand Prix due to the condition of the tarmac. By 1980 it was deemed too dangerous for car racing, although it continued to hold motorcycle racing up to 1981, when it was closed after its licence expired.

The wrecked Mercedes of Richard 'Dick' Seaman, who was leading a wet 1939 Belgian Grand Prix at Spa and crashed his car into a tree during lap 22. It was reported that on his death-bed he remarked to the Mercedes chief engineer, "I was going too fast for the conditions – it was entirely my own fault – I am sorry." He died some hours later, at the age of only 26.

The first Belgian Grand Prix was won in 1925 by Antonio Ascari. His son Alberto, seen here, won the race in 1952 and 1953. Unfortunately Antonio was killed in his next outing at the French Grand Prix. Alberto Ascari in a Ferrari 500 leads Giuseppe Farina and Jean Behra at the start of the 1952 race.

A tragic scene at the 1982 Belgian Grand Prix at Zolder: the remains of Gilles Villeneuve's totally destroyed Ferrari 126C2 chassis after his fatal accident during practice. Marshals surround Villeneuve, who was thrown from the car, receiving terrible injuries. Jochen Mass, whose car he had touched causing him to crash, stands in the middle, obviously aware of the bad news.

The start of the 1984 Belgian Grand Prix at the Zolder circuit shows Michele Alboreto in a Ferrari 126C4 leading Derek Warwick in a Renault RE50 and Rene Arnoux, also in a Ferrari. Alboreto went on to win the race.

Today it is part of an industrial park, although if you look hard it is still possible to see remnants of the old track.

Once Nivelles had closed, the Grand Prix continued to be run at Zolder, with Gunnar Nilsson scoring his first and only victory in 1977; the following year the American Mario Andretti took the chequered flag in a Lotus and in 1979 Jody Scheckter won in a Ferrari. Didier Pironi, driving a Ligier, became a first-time winner in 1980, whilst a chaotic race was won in 1981 by Carlos Reutemann. During the weekend a mechanic was killed in the pitlane, there was a drivers' strike and then a start-line accident. It seemed that things were spiralling out of control, so it was probably a good thing that the circuit at Spa, which had been going through a major overhaul, was ready to hold the Grand Prix in 1983. The race did return once more to Zolder in 1984, but from 1985 it has been held at the Spa-Francorchamps circuit.

One notable race at Spa was the 1998 Belgian Grand Prix, which took place in torrential rain, under black skies and with minimal visibility. The race even started badly, as a massive pile-up ensued at the first corner, involving thirteen of the twenty-two entrants. Later in the race, and with Michael Schumacher well in the lead, he managed to plough straight into the back of David Coulthard, who was slowing down rather suddenly, just as Schumacher was about to pass him. Many commented at the time that Schumacher didn't need to be going so fast in

Emerson Fittipaldi, already a World Champion and winner of this race, leads Niki Lauda, who would go on to be World Champion the following year, across the finishing line at the Nivelles-Baulers circuit in 1974. The Grand Prix was only run twice at the circuit.

The 1980 Belgian Grand Prix at Zolder, which was won by Didier Pironi driving a Ligier JS11/15-Ford Cosworth. He is seen here leading the pack and about to tackle Sterrewachtbocht – the first left-hander – after the start/finish line, which can be seen in the background.

By 1991 the Belgian Grand Prix was back at the magnificent Spa-Francorchamps circuit. Situated amongst the rolling hills of the Ardennes, it is easy to see from this picture why it is such a popular track. This view looking down towards Pouhon sets the scene beautifully.

It's incredible to think that Michael Schumacher, seen by many as the greatest Formula One racing driver ever, made his debut at the Spa circuit driving a Jordan 191 Ford, in 1991. Here is Schumacher negotiating La Source hairpin at that very race.

such conditions and with such a commanding lead, whilst others said that Coulthard shouldn't have slowed like that. Either way, Schumacher stormed into the McLaren garage and confronted Coulthard. Speaking at the French Grand Prix at Magny-Cours in 2003, the Scot accepted for the first time that he was to blame for the 1998 collision in Belgium, when a raging Schumacher accused the McLaren driver of trying to kill him! At the end of the day, both victory and second position went to a very under-performing Jordan team, with Damon Hill taking the flag, followed by his team-mate Ralf Schumacher.

Michael had made his debut at the Spa circuit in 1991 and the following year he won his first race there. He also won his fifty-second Grand Prix there in 2001, which saw him surpass the all-time record of fifty-one wins by Alain Prost, and as if that wasn't enough, he also won his seventh World Championship there in 2004.

With the outcry over the banning of tobacco advertising, which Formula One teams relied on heavily, new European legislation was brought in with the directive that no more tobacco advertising should be placed on the cars. Due to this political and legislatorial situation, the Grand Prix at the Spa circuit was left out of the 2003 calendar as a response to the internal tobacco legislation in Belgium. In 2004 the event was tagged as a World Class event within the national senate, and thus it was saved for the 2004 season.

That year the section known as the Bus Stop chicane was re-profiled with an additional sweep to the right. There was much speculation regarding the overtaking possibilities at the new chicane, but it seems that in racing conditions it is possible, even though a little difficult.

Schumacher won the Grand Prix in 2001 and 2002, but a new young pretender to his throne snapped it away in 2004 and 2005. The young Finn Kimi Räikkönen driving a McLaren Mercedes, crossed the finishing line ahead of Schumacher in 2004, whilst in 2005 Schumacher was hit by Takuma

The safety car leads Michael Schumacher (Benetton B195 Renault), Roberto Moreno (Forti FG01-95) and Damon Hill (Williams FW17 Renault) through the Bus Stop Chicane during a rain-soaked 1995 Belgian Grand Prix at the Spa circuit.

As cool as ever, this is Finnish driver Kimi Räikkönen guiding his McLaren Mercedes MP4/19B to the chequered flag to win the 2004 Belgian Grand Prix at Spa-Francorchamps.

Despite Kimi Räikkönen taking his and McLaren's first race win of the season, the 2004 Belgian Grand Prix belonged to Michael Schumacher – who won his seventh World Championship here – and of course to the whole Ferrari team. Evidently a good excuse to have a photo call!

This is the Le Source hairpin at the Spa circuit during lap 14 of the 2005 Belgian Grand Prix. Takuma Sato managed to drive into the back of Michael Schumacher, who was more than a little unhappy about the situation. Both drivers retired.

Sato, only to have to retire. The 2006 Formula One calendar was the same as the previous year, with the Belgian Grand Prix included. However, on February 8, the FIA announced that the Belgian National Sporting Authority (RACB) was withdrawing the Spa race from the 2006 calendar due to lack of time to complete on-going improvements. The Grand Prix was back in 2007, with much upgrading having been completed. Ferrari once again took the honours this year, with Räikkönen and Massa taking first and second place respectively. Räikkönen won again in 2009, giving him a total of four victories at the track.

If you are a seasoned camper, there is plenty of space in the surrounding wooded areas, but go prepared for rain! This is a great racing weekend and the venue is spectacular, so it is well worth a visit.

CHINESE GRAND PRIX

Venue: Shanghai International Circuit, China

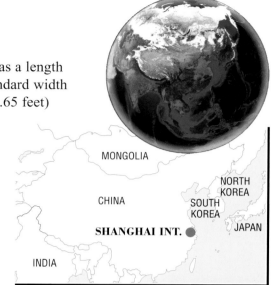

Shanghai, the venue for the Chinese Formula One Grand Prix, is situated on the banks of the Yangtze River Delta in East China. It is the largest city of the People's Republic of China and the eighth largest in the world.

The Chinese Grand Prix is a recent addition to the Formula One race calendar. It was inaugurated on 26 September 2004, the race being won by Rubens Barricello in a Ferrari. The Formula One race track has an overall length of 5.451,24 metres (17.885 feet) and includes seven left and seven right-hand turns. The longest straight runs parallel to a dragster track between turns 13 and 14, and has a length of 1.175 metres (3.854 feet). The standard width of the track is between 13 metres (42.65 feet) and 15 metres (49.21 feet), but on the corners it increases up to 20 metres (65.62 feet), as on turn 13.

Like many of the new generation race circuits, it was designed by the German architect Hermann Tilke. The design has been cleverly thought out and combines turns, straight lines and changing gradients.

Shanghai International Circuit, China

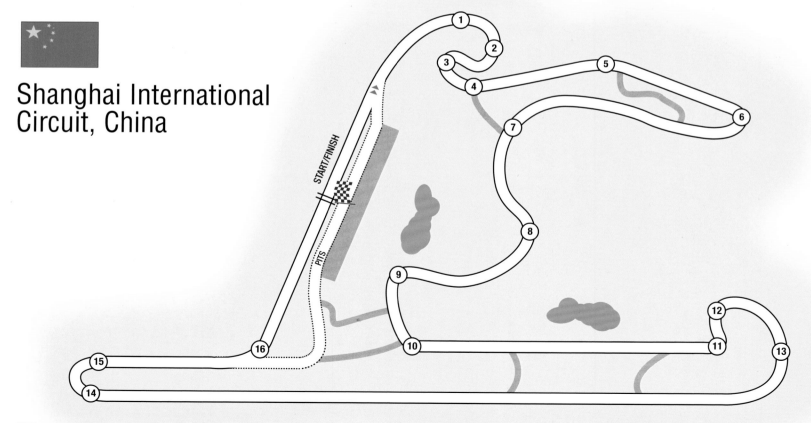

Drivers can reach a top speed of 327 kph (204.4 mph) on the longest straight – between turns 12 and 13. A maximum speed of around 87 kph (54.3 mph) is sufficient to get the cars round the tightest bends. Due to the characteristics of the circuit, there are good opportunities for overtaking, which of course adds excitement for the spectator. There has been a considerable amount of criticism in the past about the fact that the cars no longer overtake, something the FIA has attempted to address with new rules, technology and different tyres.

The 2004 Chinese Grand Prix, which took place at the Shanghai International Circuit, was the first Formula One race to be held in China. Seen here is a near-capacity crowd watching the race from one of the new grandstands opposite the pit area.

Besides the Formula One Grand Prix, there are other events that take place at the circuit. The MotoGP motorcycling event is held here, as is the Australian-based V8 championship, and recently the A1 Grand Prix also became a regular visitor along with drag racing.

The buildings and architectural features of the circuit all symbolize certain aspects of Chinese history, nature or technology. The entrance for the spectators to the grandstand is 'guarded' by two red columns and the entrance for the teams to the pit building is 'guarded' by two large glass towers. One of each type of these towers is bridged by a

Team-mates Rubens Barrichello and Jenson Button (Honda RA106) pictured on the warm-up lap during the 2006 Chinese Grand Prix. Seen in the background are the symbolic wing-shaped press centre and restaurant areas positioned over the track.

A lonely Renault makes its way from turn 16, which leads into the main grandstand area and the start/finish line. This shot from the Saturday qualifying session of the 2004 Chinese Grand Prix shows how much room there is for overtaking, although aerodynamics can play a big part in the manoeuvre.

press centre and restaurant, the shape of which is 'wing-like'. The materials used to construct this 'wing' are aluminium, glass and steel, which in turn signify ultimate technology and high speed. The colours red and gold are applied to the cylindrical roof cut-outs, using the sunlight as natural lampions and a source of light. They symbolize luck and power and if they come together, success is guaranteed. As with many buildings in China, much of the circuit and its architecture symbolize different aspects of life.

The circuit has been designed with a network of emergency routes enclosed mostly within the protected FIA fences which give easy access for the emergency vehicles. Crashed cars can be removed from the circuit with ease, without the need to close the track and with minimal disruption to the race.

Getting to the circuit is easiest by car, although selected buses will pick you up from designated points in the city and take you there. By law, when you rent a car in China you have to have a driver too, which in fact is not a bad idea as compulsory

David Coulthard (Red Bull RB2 Ferrari, left) and Nico Rosberg (Williams FW28 Cosworth) are seen along the main back straight and about to enter turn 14 at the 2006 Chinese Grand Prix.

A group of Michael Schumacher fans at the 2006 Chinese Grand Prix. I would hazard a guess that the young lady in the middle has spotted her hero!

driving tests were only introduced in 2004. For the future, there will be access by Metro – the line is in the process of being built. Once at the circuit, the best viewing point is from the grandstand. There are plenty of seats – the stand opposite the pit area alone can seat 30,000 people – and you can view about 80 per cent of the track.

An extended stay in Shanghai is recommended. Not only is there plenty to see but there are numerous hotels and restaurants to experience. Shanghai has an extensive public transportation system, boasting the world's most extensive bus system with nearly 1,000 bus lines. The Shanghai Metro (subway and elevated light rail) has five lines at present, with more planned. Shanghai has two airports: Hongqiao and Pudong International. In 2002, German Transrapid constructed the world's first commercial maglev railway in Shanghai. The line extends from Shanghai's Longyang Road subway station to Pudong International Airport. Getting around and visiting this extraordinary city should not prove a problem.

JAPANESE GRAND PRIX

Venue: Suzuka International Racing Course, Suzuka-shi, Mie-ken, Japan

RUSSIA

CHINA

NORTH KOREA

SOUTH KOREA

JAPAN

FUJI

SUZUKA

The Suzuka race circuit is seen as one of the greatest tracks in the Formula One calendar. Originally built by Honda as a test facility back in 1962, it was designed by Dutchman John Hugenholz and also incorporates a huge theme park where a big wheel dominates the Suzuka skyline.

Traditionally this Grand Prix was the last in the season, and therefore has seen many a World Championship being won – and of course lost. This in itself made the race that much more exciting, but the circuit is also known for its challenging layout. It is unique in that it is laid out in a figure-of-eight configuration, and includes two very well known corners – the high-speed 130R and the Spoon Curve.

Because of its unique layout, Suzuka is a great test of driver skill, and is classed as one of the most difficult racing circuits in the world. At the same time, it is much loved by drivers and spectators alike. The circuit is 5.807 km (3.608 miles) long and has fourteen turns and an over/underpass – reminiscent of a classic Scalextric track! Suzuka is one of the older Grand Prix circuits and one of the oldest and most famous motorsport race tracks in Japan. Following two huge accidents in early 2000, safety became a real concern, in particular at the infamous 130R turn, which many compare with the Eau Rouge curve at Spa in Belgium. Although officials had the curve redesigned, the situation

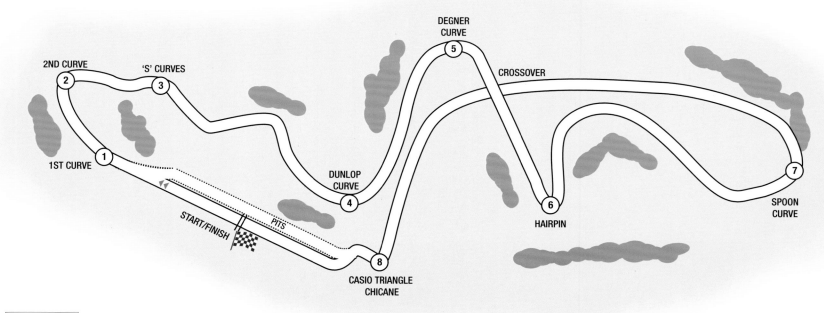

Suzuka International Racing Course, Japan

remained dangerous and, soon after, MotoGP rider Daijiro Kato was killed between 130R and the braking zone for the Casio Triangle chicane. The circuit also holds other forms of motorsport, such as the Suzuka 1000 km endurance race. It might be interesting to younger readers to know that both Suzuka and Fuji have been used on video games such as 'Pole Position II', with the Suzuka Circuit also featured in the 'Final Lap', 'Ferrari F355 Challenge' arcade games, and video games like 'Gran Turismo 4' and 'R: Racing Evolution'. Suzuka Circuit is also featured as the final race in Taito's racing game 'Continental Circus'. In 2004, the Brazilian Grand Prix was designated the last spot of the season, replacing the Japanese for that position.

The first Japanese Formula One Grand Prix took place in 1976 at the Fuji Speedway, some 40 km (25 miles) outside the city of Yokohama. There was much anticipation prior to the race as the World Championship was now on a knife-edge. James

Jenson Button (Honda RA106), seen here negotiating Casio chicane during Saturday qualifying for the 2006 Japanese Grand Prix at Suzuka. The wheel in the background is one of the many attractions found in the Motopia amusement area nearby.

Hunt, driving a McLaren, was on the verge of taking the championship from Ferrari driver Niki Lauda. Lauda had had a near-fatal accident at the German Grand Prix earlier in the year, but by a miracle had managed to get back into his racing car within months. As the weeks had ticked by, Hunt had gradually eaten away at the once hefty lead Lauda had accumulated. The outcome unfortunately was

Michael Schumacher and team-mate Felipe Massa, both in Ferrari 248 F1s, head the convoy of cars past the start/finish line and pits exit (left) at Suzuka during the 2006 race.

Sakon Yamamoto, driving a Super Aguri SA06-Honda, is pictured going under the flyover at the Suzuka circuit during Saturday practice for the 2006 Japanese Grand Prix.

Nelson Piquet, driving a Williams FW11B Honda, seen on his way to clinching the World Championship in the 1987 Grand Prix. This is a great view of the Suzuka circuit from the exit of first curve through to the 'S' curve.

Many a championship has been won and lost at the Japanese Grand Prix, but none has been quite so emotional as the 1976 one at the Fuji ciruit when Niki Lauda, having cheated death, decided to retire from the rain-soaked race. This allowed James Hunt to take third place, four points, and the championship by one point.

decided very early on when Lauda pulled out of the monsoon-hit race, pointing out that his life was more important than the championship. So Hunt went on to win the championship by a slender one point after finishing in third position. The following year an accident between Gilles Villeneuve and Ronnie Peterson ended with the death of a marshal after the Ferrari of Villeneuve somersaulted into a restricted area where he was standing. Following this accident, the Formula One race ceased to be run in Japan for a further ten years.

Fuji International Speedway, Japan

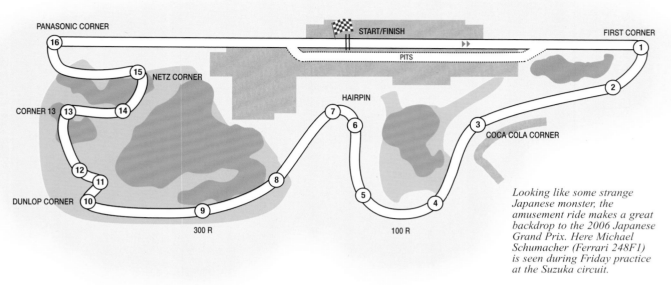

PANASONIC CORNER

START/FINISH

FIRST CORNER

16

1

PITS

15

NETZ CORNER

2

HAIRPIN

7

3

CORNER 13   13   14

6

COCA COLA CORNER

12

8

11

5

DUNLOP CORNER   10

9   4

300 R

100 R

Looking like some strange Japanese monster, the amusement ride makes a great backdrop to the 2006 Japanese Grand Prix. Here Michael Schumacher (Ferrari 248F1) is seen during Friday practice at the Suzuka circuit.

When the race did return in 1987, it was at the Suzuka International Racing Circuit located on Ise Bay on the Island of Honshu in south-central Japan, about 320 km from Tokyo. Another championship battle was raging, between Nigel Mansell, in a Williams-Honda, and his teammate, Nelson Piquet. Mansell crashed his car in practice and never started the race, handing the championship to Piquet.

One season that did catch the attention of Formula One followers was 1989, when Alain Prost and Ayrton Senna battled it out for the right to be World Champion. Again it came down to the Japanese Grand Prix to be the title decider. During the race, Senna tried to overtake Prost in an attempt to capture the lead and take the championship. Unfortunately Prost swerved into Senna, putting both men out of the race and handing the championship to Prost. Just a year later Senna returned the compliment and rammed Prost off the road, thereby securing his own championship.

As the twenty-first century kicked in, several memorable races have been run, in particular between Michael Schumacher and Mika Häkkinen. Schumacher took his first World Championship for

Mount Fuji provides one of the best backdrops for any circuit. In the foreground is the revamped Fuji Formula One circuit, now slightly different in design. The old 'Last Corner' has had an indent added, while the track and facilities have been upgraded to satisfy today's Grand Prix regulations.

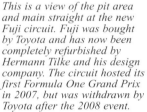

This is a view of the pit area and main straight at the new Fuji circuit. Fuji was bought by Toyota and has now been completely refurbished by Hermann Tilke and his design company. The circuit hosted its first Formula One Grand Prix in 2007, but was withdrawn by Toyota after the 2008 event.

Ferrari in 2000 and in 2003 he also managed to clinch eighth position, enough to earn him one valuable point and his sixth World Championship, thus breaking the record held by Argentinian driver Juan Manuel Fangio.

The Fuji Speedway has recently been given a grand makeover, which led to the decision to hold the race there from 2007. Fuji Speedway is situated in the foothills of Mount Fuji, which makes for a dramatic backdrop to the Grand Prix. Having been acquired by the Toyota Motor Corporation in 2000, the company won its bid to host a Grand Prix event there. The circuit was originally designed as a 4 km (2.5 mile) high-banked speedway, but money ran out and only one banking was finished. When it opened in 1965, however, it proved very dangerous, with serious accidents happening. Modifications were made in the hope of making it safer – increasing the length to 4.359 km (2.7 miles) – which was ultimately the case.

When the Grand Prix was no longer held at the circuit, Fuji continued to stage racing events, becoming a popular sports car venue. The main feature of the circuit is the 1.3 km-long straight – one of the longest of all motorsport circuits. Drag racing events have also been held here, and there was talk of holding a CART race at the circuit, but this never took place.

Despite redevelopment and the new Hermann Tilke design, Fuji was taken off the calendar after being part of the championship in 2007 and 2008 when Toyota claimed it could not afford to host it due to the global economic downturn. The Japanese Grand Prix returned to Suzuka from 2009.

BRAZILIAN GRAND PRIX

Venue: Autódromo José Carlos Pace/Interlagos, São Paulo, Brazil

The Interlagos circuit is situated just 16 km (10 miles) south of the vibrant city of São Paulo, Brazil. Rubens Barrichello, a local of this area, will tell you that even though the 'favelas' still exist, this doesn't mean it's all run-down. São Paulo is the richest state in Brazil and has the second highest per capita income, and it also shares the highest standard of living in Brazil, despite there being poverty in some peripheral parts of the largest cities. (Take, for instance, the beautiful gardens, parks and palace in São Paulo itself.) A legacy of the tragic death of Ayrton Senna, who was also a close friend of Barrichello, is the Senna foundation, which subsidises under-privileged children in the city. Lots of good things have and are happening in São Paulo, and it would be a shame not to visit this exciting city whilst you are in the area.

As for the circuit, well, race weekend is like festival time,

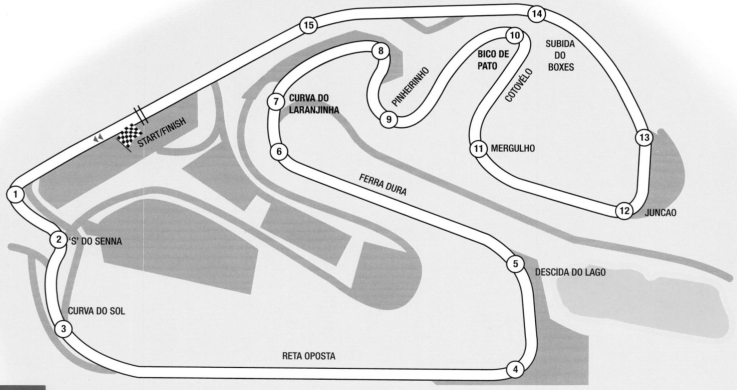

Autódromo José Carlos Pace/Interlagos, São Paulo, Brazil

Giancarlo Fisichella in his Renault R26 flashes past the newly painted shanty houses on the edge of the Interlagos circuit during the Friday practice session of the 2006 Brazilian Grand Prix.

with people coming from miles to see their local hero. Barrichello, of course, has always attracted the crowds and he is the first to appreciate their loyalty. The atmosphere on race day is full of colour, noise and spectacle – after all, you are in the land of carnivals, and the Brazilians know how to party.

The terrain where the circuit sits was originally intended to have houses built on it, but it was discovered that it was not suitable for that and so a race circuit was constructed instead. Interlagos, roughly translated, means 'between two lakes', and in fact the land where the circuit was built had two artificial lakes nearby – Guarapiranga and Billings. These were constructed to supply the city with electricity and water. In the 1970s the circuit was named after Brazilian Formula One racing driver José Carlos Pace, who had died in a plane crash. There is also a kart circuit within the grounds which is named after the great Ayrton Senna.

The sprawling suburbs near Interlagos are visible in the background as Australian Mark Webber in his Williams FW28-Cosworth pushes for position during Friday practice at the 2006 Grand Prix.

It may be Brazil but spectators come from all over the world and support all the different teams. This bunch look distinctly like Renault and Ferrari followers having a great deal of fun!

A beautiful Brazilian day at the Interlagos circuit, with a fantastic view of the 'S' bends between Cotovélo and Laranja. The rest of the circuit can be seen stretching out in the background as a McLaren leads two Jordans at the 2003 Brazilian Grand Prix.

Although it was not classified as part of the Formula One World Championship until the following year, the first Brazilian Grand Prix was held at Interlagos in 1972. The interest in racing there had been heightened when such drivers as Emmerson Fittipaldi, Carlos Reutemann and Carlos Pace became more prominent in Formula One. In 1978 the Grand Prix was moved to the Rio de Janeiro circuit, Autódromo de Jacarepaguá, which hosted the Grand Prix for one year before it returned to Interlagos. It remained there for 1979 and 1980, and then moved back to Jacarepaguá until 1990. During this period, Emmerson Fittipaldi had won races at the circuits and also managed to wrap up two world drivers' championships in 1972 and 1974. Carlos Pace had also won the race in 1975, and new boy Nelson Piquet, a local of Rio, took the spoils in 1983 and 1986 (the Jacarepaguá circuit would later be named after the Brazilian driver).

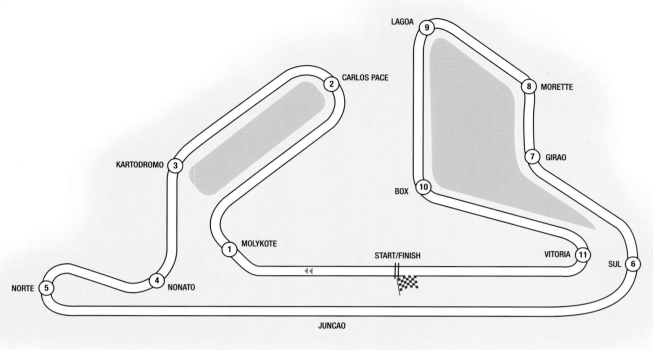

The first Brazilian Formula One Grand Prix took place at Interlagos in 1973. Local hero Emerson Fittipaldi (Lotus 72D Ford), who was then World Champion, leads team-mate Ronnie Peterson at the start of that 1973 Brazilian Grand Prix. Fittipaldi went on to win.

Autódromo Nelson Piquet, Rio de Janeiro, Brazil

The Jacarepaguá circuit was built in 1978 on reclaimed marshland, which made the circuit quite flat with little elevation change. The track consisted of two main straights plus numerous slow-speed corners. But the backdrop of the Rio mountains was enough to take your breath away. Drivers aren't there for the scenery, though, and today the circuit has been part-demolished to make way for the 2007 Pan-American games.

The race returned to Interlagos in 1990, and has remained there ever since. It is one of a handful of circuits that runs anti-clockwise – Istanbul and Imola are two other circuits that do so, and there are also some in the USA. The circuit design dates back to the 1990s, when it was shortened considerably from the original layout. It was once 7,829 metres long, whereas today it is just 4,397 metres, modified to comply with the FIA demands on track lengths. In this way it lost three long straight sections and three

fast bends. Although nobody ever perished there in a Formula One race, it was deemed too dangerous for that series of racing. The circuit still has a fast section, although it suffers from bumps, high-speed turns and a lack of run-off areas. Having said this, the drivers still love to race there and find it an interesting and demanding circuit with quite a lot of variability in the terrain. As far as facilities and organization are concerned, they can be a little

The hot air balloons give a bit of colour to the grey high-rise apartment blocks behind the Autódromo de Jacarepaguá, as Ayrton Senna starts his first race in a McLaren MP4/4 Honda. Although on pole position for the 1988 race, due to a broken gear selector mechanism he had to start in the spare car from the pits.

A scene from the 1980 Brazilian Grand Prix: René Arnoux in a Renault RE20 is making his way towards Laranjinha, as the rest of the pack negotiate the Curva do Lago at Interlagos.

Nelson Piquet in a Williams FW11B Honda leads fellow Brazilian Ayrton Senna (Lotus 99T Honda) and others at the frantic start to the 1987 Brazilian Grand Prix. The Autódromo de Jacarepaguá would later be renamed after Piquet.

Situated in one of the greenest areas around Rio and with some stunning backdrops, the Autódromo de Jacarepaguá was an enjoyable experience for drivers and spectators. Seen here is Nigel Mansell making his debut with Ferrari at the 1989 Brazilian Grand Prix.

lacking at times. For example, in 2000 during the qualifying sessions, an advertising board decided to break loose and fell on to the track. At one point it nearly hit the speeding car of Jean Alesi, who fortunately escaped unhurt. Then during the 2004 practice session a stray dog decided it would be fun to go for a stroll on the circuit and brought proceedings to a premature halt. The fact that the track itself is not in the best condition and can be very bumpy also causes some drivers to complain, although complete resurfacing work in 2007 improved the situation somewhat.

All the same, this is without doubt a great circuit and has hosted some spectacular racing over the years. One particularly interesting race took place in 2003, when several storms hit the circuit and caused all sorts of devastation and confusion. The lead

The Brazilian Formula One Grand Prix returned to Interlagos in 1990. Here, Takuma Sato (BAR Honda 007) is seen leading Jarno Trulli (Toyota TF105), Felipe Massa (Sauber Petronas C24) and Fernando Alonso (Renault) out of the start straight and towards the 'S' du Senna bends during the 2005 Brazilian Grand Prix.

No Brazilian is involved in the battle for the title, but you can bet your bottom dollar that the Brazilians will be following the championship all the way. Here hoardings announce the battle between Schumacher and Alonso at the end of the 2006 season.

changed several times, with drivers also unable to keep their machines on the track. Race leader David Coulthard decided on a pit-stop, and his team-mate Kimi Räikkönen took over the lead after fifty-three laps. A mistake by him allowed Giancarlo Fisichella to take the lead on lap fifty-four. Near the end of his fifty-fourth lap, Mark Webber crashed hard while exiting the final corner, and it was decided to bring out the safety car. However, Fernando Alonso failed to take notice of the yellow flags, and managed to clip one of Webber's stray tyres at full speed next time around – his fifty-fifth lap. At this point, safety barrier tyres spilled out all over the track, making it nearly impossible to continue the race. For safety reasons, the red flag was brought out and the race was terminated. Under Formula One regulations at the time, article 154 stated that if 75 per cent of the race distance had been completed – in this case fifty-four completed laps – it was 'deemed to have finished when the leading car crossed the line at the

end of the lap two laps prior to that lap, during which the signal to stop was given'. Therefore the stewards, believing that Fisichella was on his fifty-fifth lap – and had therefore completed the fifty-four laps required for a full result – awarded the victory to the race leader at the end of the fifty-third lap, namely Kimi Räikkönen. Several days later, and after the chaos of this extraordinary Grand Prix had died down, the official scoring evidence showed that

The 2003 Brazilian Grand Prix, Interlagos: Jarno Trulli (Renault R23) tip-toes past the wreck of his team-mate Fernando Alonso, who had crashed dramatically after clipping the tyre of Mark Webber. The race was stopped due to safety tyres spilling out all over the track.

Fisichella had just started his fifty-sixth lap before the red flag signal was given. This was meant that the race results should have been determined as of the end of lap fifty-four, not the end of lap fifty-three. So, Fisichella, who was leading after fifty-four laps, was belatedly named the winner by the FIA.

Another memorable event came in 2001 when the explosive Columbian Juan Pablo Montoya made his mark on the Formula One scene. He was on his way to winning the race but for a crash from the rear. He made up for the accident in 2004, when he did eventually win the Brazilian Grand Prix. This was in fact his last race for BMW prior to his move to McLaren. He is not only a fun person but also a very exciting driver who was prepared to mix it with the best. Several confrontations with Schumacher were a delight to watch and not too much love was lost between the two. He did liven up Formula One and many were sad to see him move away from this series of racing.

In 2005, for the first time, the Brazilian Grand Prix decided the World Championship. It was won by Fernando Alonso, who became the youngest-ever Formula One World Champion.

The 2006 season finally came to an end at the Brazilian Grand Prix. Fernando Alonso and his Renault team-mates celebrate another World Championship after their hard-fought season with Ferrari. This race was also the last to be run by for Michael Schumacher, who was retiring.

Michael Schumacher played out his last race at the 2006 Brazilian Grand Prix, and what an eventful race that was. Even though he had been robbed of a secure ten points in the previous race in Japan, due to an unexpected engine failure, he was determined to continue the fight in true Schumacher style. He was now racing against the previous year's

The McLaren MP4-23 Mercedes of Lewis Hamilton, leads Timo Glock in his Toyota TF108. Glock had the wrong set of tyres on and significantly lost speed when it started to rain and thus handed the championship to Hamilton.

champion, and possible champion-to-be, Fernando Alonso. Schumacher was fighting the odds, as he would have to win the race and see that Alonso didn't finish. All Alonso had to do was finish in a points position to secure his second championship. Schumacher drove the race of his life, finishing an incredible fourth position after starting in tenth place on the grid. A puncture had also sent him reeling to the back of the pack during the race, but he still put some stunning race times in. Unfortunately he was unable to stop Alonso from clinching his second World Championship. The eventual race winner, the new young Brazilian driver Felipe Massa, sent the crowd into a frenzy when he crossed the line, and many wondered if he would become the first Brazilian Formula One driver to clinch a World Championship since the great Ayrton Senna.

Once again the Brazilian Grand Prix was the decisive race to assertain who would become 2007 World Champion. In an incredible twist of events, rookie driver Lewis Hamilton, who held a four point lead in the championship prior to the race, suffered a series of problems and finish 7th. This lost him the championship by one point to Kimi Räikkönen, who also won the race.

The 2008 race saw Hamilton take his revenge. Massa and Hamilton had been scrapping it out for most of the second half of the season. Once again the title went down to the wire, in fact it went down to the last corner when on the rain soaked track, Hamilton managed to overtake Timo Glock, which put him into 5th place and gave him enough points to take the championship from Massa – it couldn't have been closer! Hamilton became the youngest World Champion in history at the age of 23.

The Mayor of São Paolo announced in 2008 that he had come to an agreement with Bernie Ecclestone regarding the running of the Brazilian Grand Prix. He confirmed that the agreement allowed the Grand Prix to be staged at the Interlagos circuit until 2015 but that a considerable amount of work would be carried out, in particular with the pit and paddock facilities to extend the contract.

AUSTRIAN GRAND PRIX

Venue: A1-Ring/Österreichring, Spielberg, Styria, Austria

As with so many race circuits of the period, the first Austrian Formula One Grand Prix was held at an airfield, in this case at Zeltweg in central Austria. Silverstone airfield in England was already successfully being used for racing, and it was thought that Zeltweg could also be a good venue. The 3.199 km (1.988 mile) track was prepared and the 1964 Austrian Formula One Grand Prix was scheduled to be held there in the month of August. The event was a great success and saw Lorenzo Bandini winning the race in his Ferrari, with the BRM of Richie Ginther taking second spot. Unfortunately, problems with the track surface – the fact that it was narrow and bumpy – and with spectators who complained that viewing was not great, resulted in this year being the only year that the event took place at the airfield.

It was seen as too dangerous, and so the FIA decided to remove it from the calendar until a more suitable venue could be found.

The next Austrian Formula One Grand Prix was scheduled for 1970 and would be held at the Österreichring, again located near the town of Zeltweg. The track was 4.326 km (2.684 miles) long, and with a total of ten corners was seen as both challenging and dangerous, with some very demanding, tight corners and long fast straights with dramatic elevation changes. There was little in the way of run-off areas, and four-times, world champion Alain Prost commented that the circuit should not be changed but have new run-off areas added to make it safer. There are two particularly dangerous corners around the circuit, the 180-degree 'Boschkurve' and the 'Hella-Licht', which unfortunately is where American driver Mark Donahue was to have a tragic and ultimately fatal accident in 1975.

The circuit hosted the Grand Prix for the next seventeen years, and during this time it saw some

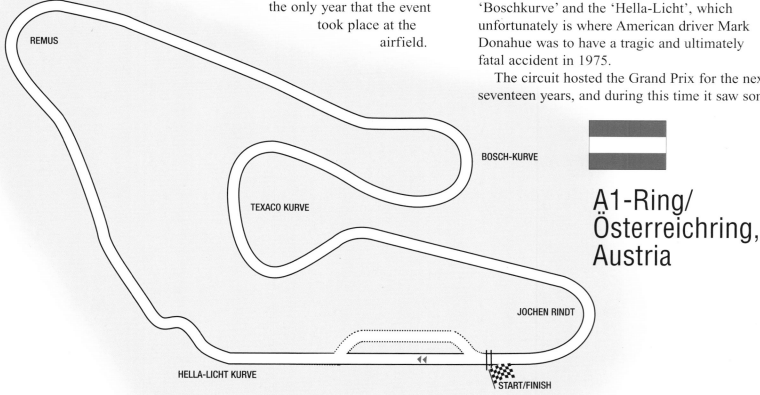

REMUS

BOSCH-KURVE

TEXACO KURVE

JOCHEN RINDT

HELLA-LICHT KURVE

START/FINISH

A1-Ring/ Österreichring, Austria

great races with quite often some very unpredictable winners. The first race, run over sixty laps, was won by Jacki Ickx in a Ferrari, with his teammate Clay Regazzoni taking second place just .61 seconds behind him. The following year saw the emergence of another great Austrian, Niki Lauda, who went on to win two World Championships in the 1970s with

Ferrari. A rain-drenched circuit saw the race being stopped on lap twenty-nine in 1975. Vittorio Brambilla was leading at the time and therefore was awarded the race, even though he managed to crash the car whilst crossing the line. The 1980 race was eventful for being the tightest finish on record for a Formula One race. A mere .82 seconds separated

The stunning Österreichring hosted the Formula One Austrian Grand Prix for eighteen consecutive years up to 1987. It was then shortened, rebuilt and renamed A1-Ring, and again hosted races from 1997 through 2003. Here, race leader Rubens Barrichello (Ferrari F2001) leads the pack during the 2001 race.

Jean-Pierre Jabouille from Alan Jones, with Jabouille taking the win in his Renault. Then just two years on, even this was beaten when Elio de Angelis beat Keke Rosberg by .125 seconds, to give him his first Formula One Grand Prix win. The 1987 Austrian Grand Prix turned out to be something of a disaster, with three starts needed and several other incidents. Although nobody got hurt, it was decided to replace the race with the Hungarian event.

When the teams finally returned in 1997, the circuit had been totally rebuilt by none other than Hermann Tilke and his design group. Now renamed the A1-Ring, the track was shortened to 4.326 km (2.684 miles) and the fast sweeping corners were replaced by three tight right-handers to create overtaking opportunities. There is no question regarding the safety of the track, but many argued that its soul had been taken away. So from 1998 through to 2003, the Austrian Grand Prix was held there. In 2002, the race received some very negative publicity when Ferrari instructed Rubens Barricello, whilst clearly leading the race, to make way for

Michael Schumacher. This infuriated fans and the Press and eventually led to the banning of team orders which 'artificially' determined the outcome of a race. The last Grand Prix was run there in 2003, won again by Michael Schumacher in a Ferrari, ahead of Kimi Räikkönen in a McLaren Mercedes.

Niki Lauda, driving a Ferrari 312T2, leads his home Grand Prix at the start of the 1977 race at the Österreichring. He would go on to win his second World Championship and leave Ferrari at the end of this season.

The 1964 Austrian Grand Prix at the Österreichring: Lorenzo Bandini (Ferrari 156), definitely trying hard and willing the car to keep right. This was his maiden and only Grand Prix win. Note the lack of barriers and the straw bale!

Quite clearly marked on the verge is the new name of the circuit, as Michael Schumacher (Ferrari F2003 GA) flashes past during qualifying for the 2003 Austrian Grand Prix.

DUTCH GRAND PRIX

Venue: Circuit Park Zandvoort, Zandvoort, Netherlands

Although there were already two motorcycle race circuits being used in the Netherlands in the 1930s, Drenthe and Limburg, serious plans were afoot to create a new circuit for motor racing. So it was that on 3 June 1939 car racing was held on a road circuit near Zandvoort. Unfortunately the Second World War intervened and all racing was stopped until hostilities were over. With the success of car racing prior to the war a new circuit was opened on the sand dunes of Zandvoort on 7 August 1948.

The design of circuits today is left to a computer program; Zandvoort on the other hand was based on tracks made and used by the German Wehrmacht during the war. These tracks were used to connect the shore batteries. The new track was devised by a group of Dutch motorcycle enthusiasts, who were advised by the 1927 Le Mans 24 Hours winner, Sammy Davis. Because of the sand dunes, the track was undulating and the elevation changed regularly, in particular on the Scheivlak corner, which went downhill and to the right. The most famous corner and well known to the older generation, was the Tarzan corner, which is situated at the end of the pit straight.

In 1949 the circuit hosted the Zandvoort Grand Prix, which became the Dutch Grand Prix in 1950.

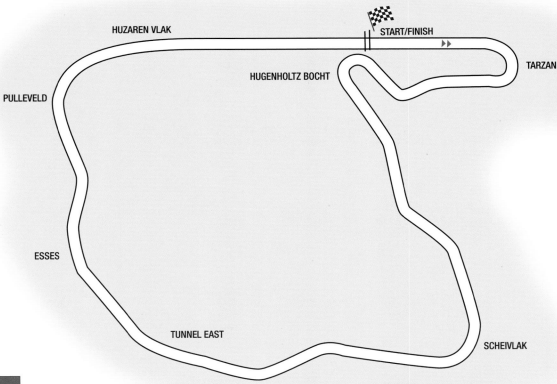

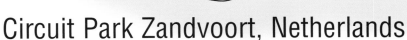

Circuit Park Zandvoort, Netherlands

It wasn't until 1952 that it gained official Formula One Grand Prix status and the first World Championship race was run there. A variety of cars were entered for the race: Ferrari, Gordini, Cooper-Bristol, Maserati and many more. With Ferrari dominating at the time, Alberto Ascari won the race, followed up by two other Ferraris, with 1953 seeing a similar story. There was no race in 1954, but it did return in 1955, despite the Le Mans tragedy and cancellation of all other races. Zandvoort joined the list of cancellations in 1956 and 1957 but returned again in 1958, when it was run annually and uninterrupted until 1971. Again a year was missed and racing then continued from 1973 through to 1985, when it was stopped for good.

When racing returned in 1958, Stirling Moss won in a front-engined Vanvall, while 1960 saw the debut of Jim Clark, who immediately gave Graham Hill a thing or two to think about before having to retire. For 1961, Phil Hill, in the famous

Jack Brabham (Brabham BT19-Repco) leads Jim Clark (Lotus 33-Climax), Denny Hulme (Brabham BT20-Repco) and the rest of the pack early in the 1966 Dutch Grand Prix. Brabham went on to win the race.

An incredible period photograph, showing a scene during the 1966 Dutch Grand Prix at the Zandvoort circuit. Mechanics are seen working on the Cooper T81 Maserati of John Surtees prior to the race.

There was no racing in 1972 due to lack of funds to improve the circuit, but that was remedied and crash barriers were erected all around the track, while a new speed control section was added at the rear of the circuit, the Panoramabocht. New pits and VIP areas were also created. Racing returned to Zandvoort in 1973 after all this improvement, but on lap eight, Roger Williamson hit one of the new Armco barriers, which sent his car into the air. It landed on the track, upside down and in flames. His close friend David Purley stopped his car and tried to free the trapped Williamson, but in vain. The late 1970s saw Mario Andretti and Alan Jones not only win at Zandvoort but the championship too. In the 1980s, Lauda won a third championship and Prost won his first, the two combining their talents with the McLaren team. In recent years the circuit has taken on major redevelopment and although the Formula One fraternity do not visit anymore, Circuit Park Zandvoort played host to the first race in the 2006/2007 season of A1 Grand Prix races, and continues to do so. 2009 also saw the return of the Masters of Formula 3 race series to the circuit, but there is no talk of Formula One returning yet.

The 1985 Dutch Grand Prix at Zandvoort was the last time Formula One would visit the circuit. It was also Niki Lauda's final Formula One victory. Here he is seen driving a McLaren MP4/2B TAG Porsche and being hounded by Ayrton Senna's Lotus.

shark-nosed Ferrari and on his way to his World Championship, finished second to team-mate Wolfgang Von Trips by less than a second. Jim Clark, Jackie Stewart, Jochen Rindt, Graham Hill and Jack Brabham all won races in the following years in various combinations of Lotus, Brabham, and Matra chassis cars with BRM, Climax, Repco and Ford engines. This was a time when Formula One racing was at its best, with drivers at their limit and always aware of the possible tragic consequences of an accident. Tragedy struck in 1970, when Piers Courage, heir to the giant brewing concern, crashed his car heavily. The car overturned and burst into flames, killing the driver.

SOUTH AFRICAN GRAND PRIX

Venue: Kyalami Grand Prix Circuit, Gauteng, South Africa

In its day the South African Formula One Grand Prix was one of the most popular, but over the years suffered from both governmental politics and racing politics. There have been some extraordinary races though, and although Kyalami became the main venue for the Formula One Grand Prix, the East London circuit also had its day.

Initially run as a Grand Prix handicap race in 1934 at the Prince George Circuit at East London in the Eastern Cape Province, it attracted the top drivers of the day such as Bernd Rosemeyer, Richard 'Dick' Seaman and 'Gigi' Villoresi, who won the race.

The Prince George circuit was 3.920 km (2.436 miles) long, and was inaugurated in 1930. It staged the race for a further four years from 1936 to 1939 before the Second World War intervened and all racing was stopped. The circuit was then rebuilt in 1959 to meet Formula One regulations, after which it hosted three official Formula One Grand Prix races, in 1962, 1963 and 1965. It was then seen as being too small to stage the Grand Prix, and so racing was moved to the Kyalami circuit in 1967.

The original Kyalami circuit, which was used until political sanctions eliminated the Grand Prix

 Kyalami Grand Prix Circuit, South Africa

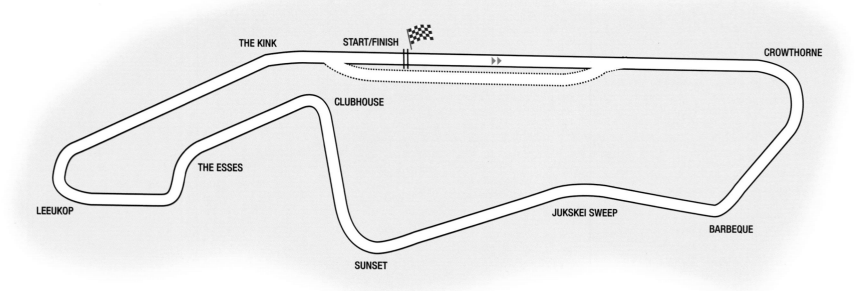

A scene from the start of the 1963 South African Grand Prix at the East London circuit: smoke and dust fly as Jim Clark (Lotus 25-Climax), Jack Brabham (Brabham BT7-Climax) and Dan Gurney (Brabham BT7-Climax) lead off the front row of the grid. Clark and Gurney finished in first and second position respectively.

in 1986, was a wonderful sweeping circuit with a variety of fast and medium-speed corners. It was 3.6 km (2.25 miles) long, and these characteristics made it not only challenging for the drivers but entertaining for the spectators too. Kyalami, with its ideal weather, was always a popular venue for off-season testing too. With Johannesburg just sixteen miles away and Pretoria a mere ten miles

away, there was never any shortage of local support, although many people came from much further afield too. A total of twenty-three Formula One Grand Prix races were held at the Kyalami track between 1962 and the final event in 1993. The 1981 event was marred by the FISA-FOCA dispute and only the teams that belonged to FOCA actually entered the race.

SOUTH AFRICAN GRAND PRIX

The circuit was rebuilt in the early 1990s and some pretty major changes took place. World-famous landmarks like Crowthorn bend, Barbeque and Jukskei sweep were either eliminated or so heavily modified they became unrecognizable. In its time Kyalami was one of the fastest circuits around; unfortunately it seems to have lost that edge and many will say that it has also lost all its character. Formula One finally stopped attending the rebuilt Kyalami circuit in 1993, and there seem to be no future plans afoot, although the circuit did stage a round of the prestigious World Superbike series from 1998 to 2002.

In 2009 a round of the A1 GP series of races was run at the Kyalami circuit, for the very first time. Although there has been no Formula One race since 1993, there are whispers of reviving the Grand Prix, possibly with a new circuit at Kyalami.

Ayrton Senna (McLaren MP4/8 Ford) leads Alain Prost (Williams FW15C Renault) and Michael Schumacher (Benetton B192B Ford) over the start/finish line at Kyalami during the 1993 South African Grand Prix.

The Kyalami circuit was a popular venue for both drivers and spectators and became the main venue for the race. Denny Hulme in a Brabham BT20 Repco is seen here at the 1967 South African Grand Prix.

A young Jody Scheckter, who became World Champion in 1979 whilst driving for the Ferrari team. He was born in South Africa and drove for the McLaren, Tyrrell, Wolf and Ferrari teams during his career in Formula One.

SWEDISH GRAND PRIX

Venue: Anderstorp Raceway, Anderstorp, Sweden

The Scandinavian Raceway, to give it its former title, is about 30 km from Jönköping, in Småland, Sweden. Otherwise known simply as Anderstorp – after the town where it is situated – the track was built on marshlands back in 1968. By the 1970s it had grown in popularity, and with the success of Swedish Formula One motor racing driver, Ronnie Peterson, the Swedish Grand Prix was staged there from 1973 to 1978. Like many race circuits of the period, the long straight – called flight straight – was also used as a runway for aircraft to take off and land on. As well as the straight, the circuit comprised several corners some of which were banked. The circuit was to hold only six World Championship Grand Prix races; the deaths of Peterson and another well-known Swedish Formula

One racing driver, Gunnar Nilsson, would restore the lack of interest that existed prior to these two local heroes becoming household names. Although there has not been another Formula One Grand Prix staged there since 1978 (and there probably never will be) during the 1980s it hosted Touring Car races and today the circuit is used for popular club events.

The first Swedish Formula One Grand Prix was run on 17 June 1973, with local boy Peterson thrilling the crowds with his exciting driving and a pole position for the race. It looked like he would crown the weekend with a win in the race too but for Denny Hulme, who overtook Peterson and his tyre-troubled Lotus on the penultimate lap, going on to win the race. This would be the closest any Swedish driver would get to winning a Swedish Grand Prix in

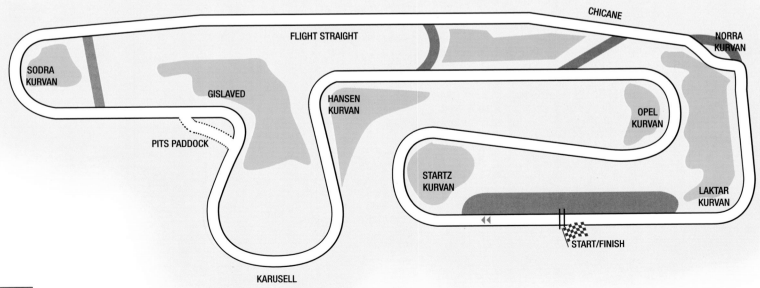

Anderstorp Raceway, Sweden

front of his home crowd. The following year Jody Scheckter won his first-ever Grand Prix at the circuit in a very dominant Tyrrell-Cosworth 007. In 1975 Niki Lauda would take Anderstorp as his third win towards a runaway World Championship in a Ferrari 312T. His teammate Clay Regazzoni drove the second Ferrari to third position, with Carlos Reutemann in his Brabham finishing second,

sandwiched between the two Ferraris. The unique six-wheeled Tyrrell P34, driven by South African Jody Scheckter, won the race in 1976, with its stablemate, driven by Patrick Depailler, coming a confident second. Strangely, the cars never won another race after this. For 1977 it was France, France, France! It was the first time that a French car (Ligier) with a French engine (Matra), backed

Ronnie Peterson's success with Team Lotus was the catalyst for a Swedish Grand Prix, with the race being held for the first time in 1973 at the Anderstorp Raceway. Unfortunately, tyre wear relegated the Swedish driver to second position at the finish.

by a French company (Gitanes), and driven by a French driver (Jacques Laffite) had won a Grand Prix – sadly it wasn't the French Grand Prix. 1978 was the last year of the Grand Prix and was marked by a very unfamiliar car, the Brabham 'fancar', as it became known. It had a huge fan on the back which, although used for cooling, also contributed to the ground effects, making the car stick to the tarmac with a vengeance. Once again Niki Lauda was the driver and he went on to win by some thirty-four seconds. All sorts of protests were mounted but the result was left to stand.

It was also this year that Ronnie Peterson was killed and Gunnar Nilsson died, which contributed to the demise of Formula One Grand Prix racing in Sweden. Peterson was badly hurt at Monza, taken to hospital and tragically died there – the cause of death being given as fat embolism. It is thought that he may have lived had the accident crew turned up quicker. For 1978 Gunnar Nilsson had signed for the Arrows team, but he was never well enough to drive the car – he died later that year of testicular cancer. A sad end to both drivers and circuit.

The 1974 Swedish Grand Prix at Anderstorp was totally dominated by the two Tyrrell-Ford 007s of Jody Scheckter and Patrick Depailler. Seen here in the pits is Scheckter, who went on to win his first-ever Grand Prix.

The big debate at the 1978 Swedish Grand Prix was not so much the race itself but the 'fancar' (Brabham BT46B Alfa Romeo) being driven by Niki Lauda and John Watson. Lauda finished first but is seen here behind Mario Andretti (Lotus 79 Ford) at the start.

CIRCUITS THAT HAVE HELD FORMULA ONE RACES SINCE 1950

Circuit	Grand Prix	Years
A1-Ring	Austrian Grand Prix	1997–2003
Adelaide Street Circuit	Australian Grand Prix	1985–1995
Ain-Diab	Moroccan Grand Prix	1958
Aintree	British Grand Prix	1955, 1957, 1959, 1961–1962
Albert Park	Australian Grand Prix	1996–
AVUS	German Grand Prix	1959
Bahrain International	Bahrain Grand Prix	2004–2010, 2012–
Circuito da Boavista	Portuguese Grand Prix	1958, 1960
Brands Hatch	British Grand Prix and European Grand Prix	1964, 1966, 1968, 1970, 1972, 1974, 1976, 1978, 1980, 1982–1986
Circuit Bremgarten	Swiss Grand Prix	1950–1954
Buddh International Circuit	Indian Grand Prix	2011–
Bugatti Circuit Le Mans	French Grand Prix	1967
Caesar's Palace	Las Vegas Grand Prix	1981–1982
Circuit of the Americas	US Grand Prix	2012–
Circuit de Catalunya	Spanish Grand Prix	1991–
Circuit Charade	French Grand Prix	1965, 1969–1970, 1972
Detroit Street Circuit	US Grand Prix East	1982–1988
Dijon-Prenois	French Grand Prix and Swiss Grand Prix	1974, 1977, 1979, 1981–1982, 1984
Donington Park	European Grand Prix	1993
Autodromo Enzo e Dino Ferrari	San Marino Grand Prix and Italian Grand Prix	1980–2006
Autódromo do Estoril	Portuguese Grand Prix	1984–1996
Fair Park Dallas	US Grand Prix	1984
Fuji Speedway	Japanese Grand Prix	1976–1977, 2007–2008
Circuit Gilles Villeneuve	Canadian Grand Prix	1978–1986, 1988–2008, 2010–
Autódromo Hermanos Rodríguez	Mexican Grand Prix	1963–1970, 1986–1992
Hockenheimring	German Grand Prix	1970, 1977–2006, 2008, 2010, 2012
Hungaroring	Hungarian Grand Prix	1986–
Indianapolis Motor Speedway	US Grand Prix	1950–1960, 2000–2007
Istanbul Park	Turkish Grand Prix	2005–2011
Autódromo Internacional Nelson Piquet	Brazilian Grand Prix	1978, 1981–1989
Circuito Permanente Del Jarama	Spanish Grand Prix	1968, 1970, 1972, 1974, 1976–1979, 1981
Circuito Permanente de Jerez	Spanish Grand Prix and European Grand Prix	1986–1990, 1994, 1997
Autódromo José Carlos Pace	Brazilian Grand Prix	1973–1977, 1979–1980, 1990–
Korea International Circuit	Korean Grand Prix	2010–
Kyalami Circuit	South African Grand Prix	1967–1980, 1982–1985, 1992–1993
Long Beach Street Circuit	US Grand Prix West	1976–1983
Magny-Cours Circuit	French Grand Prix	1991–2008
Marina Bay Street Circuit	Singaporean Grand Prix	2008–
Circuit de Monaco	Monaco Grand Prix	1950, 1955–
Monsanto Park	Portuguese Grand Prix	1959
Montjuïc Circuit	Spanish Grand Prix	1969, 1971, 1973, 1975
Mont-Tremblant	Canadian Grand Prix	1968, 1970
Autodromo Nazionale Monza	Italian Grand Prix	1950–1979, 1981–
Mosport Park	Canadian Grand Prix	1967, 1969, 1971–1977
Nivelles-Baulers Circuit	Belgian Grand Prix	1972, 1974
Nürburgring	German Grand Prix, European Grand Prix and Luxembourg Grand Prix	1951–1958, 1961–1969, 1971–1976, 1984–1985, 1995–2007, 2009, 2011, 2013
Autódromo Oscar Alfredo Gálvez	Argentine Grand Prix	1953–1958, 1960, 1972–1975, 1977–1981, 1995–1998
Österreichring	Austrian Grand Prix	1970–1987
Circuit Paul Ricard	French Grand Prix	1971, 1973, 1975–1976, 1978, 1980, 1982–1983, 1985–1990
Pedralbes Circuit	Spanish Grand Prix	1951, 1954
Pescara Circuit	Pescara Grand Prix	1957
Phoenix Street Circuit	US Grand Prix	1989–1991
Prince George Circuit	South African Grand Prix	1962–1963, 1965
Reims-Gueux	French Grand Prix	1950–1951, 1953–1954, 1956, 1958–1961, 1963, 1966
Riverside International Raceway	US Grand Prix	1960
Rouen-Les-Essarts	French Grand Prix	1952, 1957, 1962, 1964, 1968
Scandinavian Raceway	Swedish Grand Prix	1973–1978
Sebring Raceway	US Grand Prix	1959
Sepang International Circuit	Malaysian Grand Prix	1999–
Shanghai International Circuit	Chinese Grand Prix	2004–
Silverstone Circuit	British Grand Prix	1950–1954, 1956, 1958, 1960, 1963, 1965, 1967, 1969, 1971, 1973, 1975, 1977, 1979, 1981, 1983, 1985, 1987–
Spa-Francorchamps	Belgian Grand Prix	1950–1970, 1983, 1985–2002, 2004–2005, 2007–
Suzuka Circuit	Japanese Grand Prix	1987–2006, 2009–
Tanaka International Circuit	Pacific Grand Prix	1994–1995
Valencia Street Circuit	European Grand Prix	2008–
Watkins Glen	US Grand Prix	1961–1980
Yas Marina Circuit	Abu Dhabi Grand Prix	2009–
Circuit Park Zandvoort	Dutch Grand Prix	1952–1953, 1955, 1958–1971, 1973–1985
Zeltweg Airfield	Austrian Grand Prix	1964
Circuit Zolder	Belgian Grand Prix	1973, 1975–1982, 1984

DRIVERS CHAMPIONSHIP

Year	Driver	Constructor	Year	Driver	Constructor	Year	Driver	Constructor
1950	Nino Farina	Alfa Romeo	1971	Jackie Stewart	Tyrrell	1993	Alain Prost	Williams
1951	Juan Manuel Fangio	Alfa Romeo	1972	Emerson Fittipaldi	Lotus	1994	Michael Schumacher	Benetton
1952	Alberto Ascari	Ferrari	1973	Jackie Stewart	Tyrrell	1995	Michael Schumacher	Benetton
1953	Alberto Ascari	Ferrari	1974	Emerson Fittipaldi	McLaren	1996	Damon Hill	Williams
1954	Juan Manuel Fangio	Maserati, Mercedes	1975	Niki Lauda	Ferrari	1997	Jacques Villeneuve	Williams
			1976	James Hunt	McLaren	1998	Mika Häkkinen	McLaren
1955	Juan Manuel Fangio	Mercedes	1977	Niki Lauda	Ferrari	1999	Mika Häkkinen	McLaren
1956	Juan Manuel Fangio	Ferrari	1978	Mario Andretti	Lotus	2000	Michael Schumacher	Ferrari
1957	Juan Manuel Fangio	Maserati	1979	Jody Scheckter	Ferrari	2001	Michael Schumacher	Ferrari
1958	Mike Hawthorn	Ferrari	1980	Alan Jones	Williams	2002	Michael Schumacher	Ferrari
1959	Jack Brabham	Cooper	1981	Nelson Piquet	Brabham	2003	Michael Schumacher	Ferrari
1960	Jack Brabham	Cooper	1982	Keke Rosberg	Williams	2004	Michael Schumacher	Ferrari
1961	Phil Hill	Ferrari	1983	Nelson Piquet	Brabham	2005	Fernando Alonso	Renault
1962	Graham Hill	BRM	1984	Niki Lauda	McLaren	2006	Fernando Alonso	Renault
1963	Jim Clark	Lotus	1985	Alain Prost	McLaren	2007	Kimi Räikkönen	Ferrari
1964	John Surtees	Ferrari	1986	Alain Prost	McLaren	2008	Lewis Hamilton	McLaren
1965	Jim Clark	Lotus	1987	Nelson Piquet	Williams	2009	Jenson Button	Brawn
1966	Jack Brabham	Brabham	1988	Ayrton Senna	McLaren	2010	Sebastian Vettel	Red Bull
1967	Denny Hulme	Brabham	1989	Alain Prost	McLaren	2011	Sebastian Vettel	Red Bull
1968	Graham Hill	Lotus	1990	Ayrton Senna	McLaren	2012	Sebastian Vettel	Red Bull
1969	Jackie Stewart	Matra	1991	Ayrton Senna	McLaren			
1970	Jochen Rindt	Lotus	1992	Nigel Mansell	Williams			

CONSTRUCTORS CHAMPIONSHIP (Awarded from 1958)

Year	Constructor	Year	Constructor	Year	Constructor	Year	Constructor
1958	Vanwall	1972	Lotus Ford	1986	Williams Honda	2000	Ferrari
1959	Cooper Climax	1973	Lotus Ford	1987	Williams Honda	2001	Ferrari
1960	Cooper Climax	1974	McLaren Ford	1988	McLaren Honda	2002	Ferrari
1961	Ferrari	1975	Ferrari	1989	McLaren Honda	2003	Ferrari
1962	BRM	1976	Ferrari	1990	McLaren Honda	2004	Ferrari
1963	Lotus Climax	1977	Ferrari	1991	McLaren Honda	2005	Renault
1964	Ferrari	1978	Lotus Ford	1992	Williams Renault	2006	Renault
1965	Lotus Climax	1979	Ferrari	1993	Williams Renault	2007	Ferrari
1966	Brabham Repco	1980	Williams Ford	1994	Williams Renault	2008	Ferrari
1967	Brabham Repco	1981	Williams Ford	1995	Benetton Renault	2009	Brawn
1968	Lotus Ford	1982	Ferrari	1996	Williams Renault	2010	Red Bull
1969	Matra Ford	1983	Ferrari	1997	Williams Renault	2011	Red Bull
1970	Lotus Ford	1984	McLaren TAG	1998	McLaren Mercedes	2012	Red Bull
1971	Tyrrell Ford	1985	McLaren TAG	1999	Ferrari		

INDEX

ACKNOWLEDGEMENTS

The author and the publisher would like to thank
the following for all their help and support:

Majority of pictures supplied by:
LAT Photographic, London, England
With special thanks to Zoe Mayho

Other photographic contributors:
Corbis (pp73t, 73b)
Tilke GmbH & Co. KG., Germany
Julian Smallshaw collection
Singapore GP Pte Ltd
FIAT (UK)

World maps:
Copyright © 2001 United States Government as represented by the
Administrator of the National Aeronautics and Space Administration.
All rights reserved.

Circuit maps:
Bacroom Design & Advertising, Birmingham, England
Chensie Chen, Wiltshire, England
Rob Highton (p48)